Jan,

Lue Lang;

End of Tracks

Other Books by Stan Moore

OVER THE DAM
Mik Mas uncovers and works to stop eco-vigilantes in today's
Summit County, Colorado.
Fiction (overthedam.com)

SEESAW: HOW NOVEMBER '42 SHAPED THE FUTURE
A fresh look at the crux month of WWII.
Nonfiction (seesaw1942.com)

MISTER MOFFAT'S ROAD
A historical novel about David Moffat's railroad from Den-
ver towards Salt Lake City, set in 1902. Mik Mas and friends help
Moffat to overcome unforeseen barriers.

MISTER MOFFAT'S HILL
A historical novel, 1904–08 Colorado.
Cam Braun and Mik Mas struggle to run trains over the
continental divide's Rollins Pass. A diamond mine scheme comes
to their attention and fireworks result.

MISTER MOFFAT'S OPUS
A historical novel set in 1917–1929 Colorado. Political
maneuvering and financial shenanigans underlie the Moffat Tunnel railroad project. It took five years to build, cost millions, and
was the largest construction project in the nation. Mik Mas and
Cam Braun are in the thick of the effort.

MISTER HAMLIN'S LIST
A historical novel set in 1900s Cripple Creek, the 'Greatest
Gold Camp on Earth.' Follow Ben McNall, a union miner who falls
for a woman mine owner. There is violence between the union,
owners, strike breakers and the Colorado Militia. Ultimately many
people leave town, some voluntarily and some are deported.

GENERAL PEARSON'S SHIP
a novel
Around 1900, the British Army was buying lots of
American horses for their Boer War. Gace McNall and
friends are swept up. The turmoil of the foreign purchases
leads to resistance by Americans and others.

KATIE RIDES ALONE
a childrens' book
Katie is a ranch girl too young and short to reach the
stirrups while in the saddle. Ride along as she has adventures
and challenges on the way to visit Grandma and Grandpa.

End of Tracks

Stan Moore

End of Tracks is a work of fiction. Resemblance of any character to persons living or dead is purely coincidental.

I offer heartfelt thanks to the many people who helped with this book in all phases of its creation. They are too many to mention. And a special shout out to my wife Kiki for cover art, support and encouragement.

Any errors or inaccuracies are the sole property of the author.

Design by Jack Lenzo

This work is in honor of the memory of
Charles Pruden and Jenny Pruden. They were early
Colorado cattle ranchers and entrepreneurs.
They are great grandparents that I never got to meet.

Contents

Ben's Maps

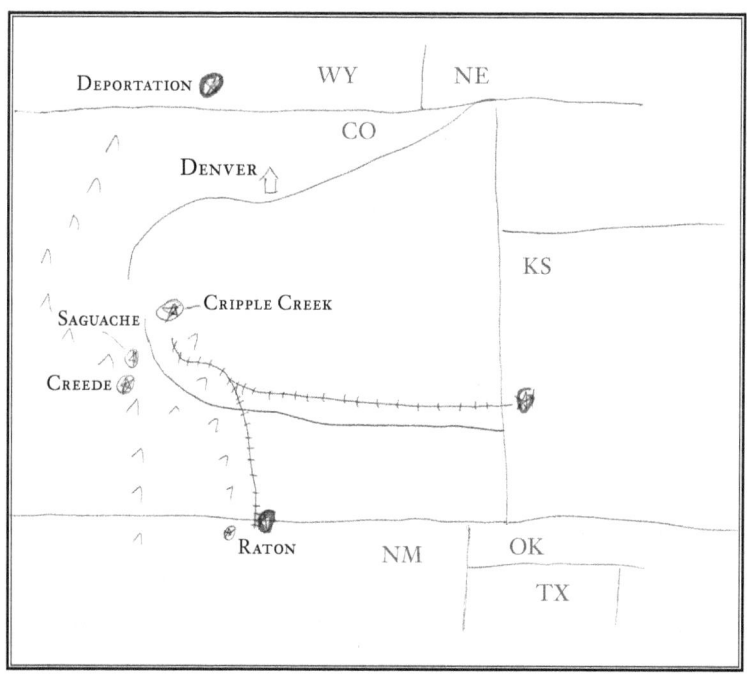

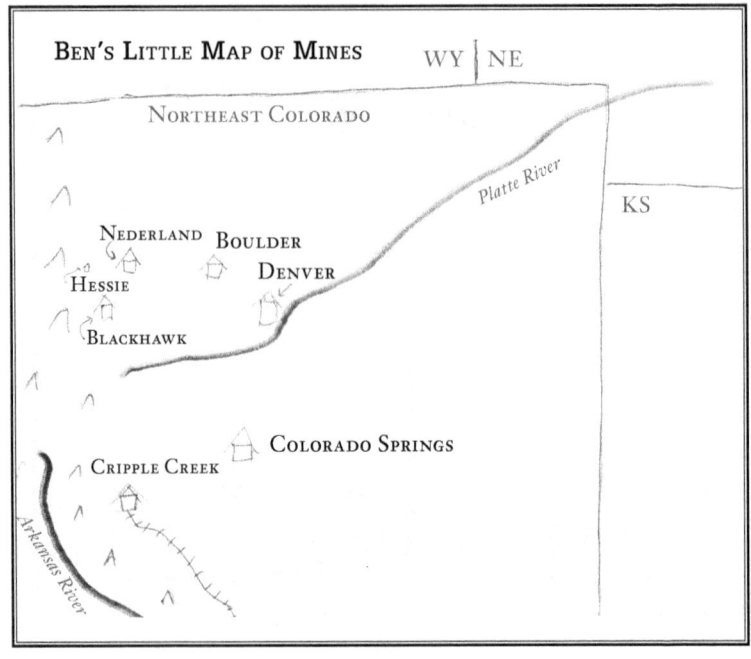

Ben's Little Map of Mines

WY | NE

Northeast Colorado

Platte River

KS

Nederland   Boulder
Hessie   Denver
Blackhawk

Colorado Springs
Cripple Creek

Arkansas River

Who Is Who in
End of Tracks

ACTUAL PEOPLE:
Ted Moore. A power line technician, surveyor, rancher, and electrician. Ted was the author's grandfather.

George Henderson. A young man swept up in the Cripple Creek labor wars. Along with twelve other miners he was killed in an explosion set off by union sympathizers. He was the author's great uncle.

OTHER CHARACTERS:
Ben McNall. Ben was a silver miner who went to mining gold in Cripple Creek.

Carlton Orville Weston the third. Goes by the name of Cow. Son of an industrialist, he escaped the east and came to Cripple to mine.

Suze Weston. Cow's wife.

Mr. and Mrs. Cobbson. A farming and 'ranching' couple on the border of Colorado and New Mexico

Abby Bosini. A Cripple Creek school teacher, she is Ben's flame and future wife.

Lon Bosini. Abby's brother, an entrepreneur and manager of the mine the siblings own together.

Gace McNall. Ben's brother, a one time silver miner now working the horse trade in Denver.

George Mason. A coworker and friend of Ben and Abby.

Paul Sawyer. A Denver businessman and promoter. In a previous life he went by Piers Sawicki.

Prologue

CRIPPLE CREEK, COLORADO JUNE 1904. A WEEK AFTER THE explosion at the Independence Station which killed thirteen, injuring many more.

BEN REACHED FOR ABBY. THEIR OUTSTRETCHED HANDS touched. Each would swear they felt a spark. Even under a hot summer sun that day high in the mountains.

She kept her voice neutral. "You don't have to do this, Ben. You don't have to be a martyr. Big Bill Haywood and the Western Federation of Miners sure don't care about you. The mine owners just want troublemakers gone, want calm and quiet. Stay. Turn your back on Haywood and his goons. Join us at the mine. We will sort things out."

Abby Bosini was a teacher at Cripple Creek school. She and her brother Lon shared ownership of a local mine, the Double I. The name paid tribute to their Italian and Irish heritage.

A militiaman's bayonet touched Ben's backside, not gently. The man's bawled orders, harsh and peremptory. "Get on the train boy."

The touching hands parted unwillingly. "I can't turn away, Abby. It isn't right how miners are treated."

Her voice, distressed and loud as he was pushed away, "Maybe. But you can't change it alone. Stay and we will work on it. I love you Ben. Stay please!"

He concentrated on climbing the step. Moved just fast enough to keep the bayonet point from piercing his skin. Its point ripped his denims as he stepped up. Ben barely heard her.

On board, he turned and their eyes locked. "I will reach you. I love…" The door slammed. She wasn't sure what he said, what she heard.

SEVERAL WEEKS PASSED. BEN WAS NOT IN COLORADO. THAT HE knew. But just where, and where he was going from here, he was not at all sure. He sketched a map on a piece of paper, just to keep his thoughts straight.

"THOSE DAMNED MINE OWNERS AND THEIR LISTS. I TELL YOU, Cow, they are chasing me to death. Us to death."

Cow spat. "Hell, Ben. The Cripple Creek Mine Owners are just a chapter in the mine owners' fraternity. Those rich owners are tight as thieves. Clarence Hamlin, their 'secretary' is just a glorified clerk. And his list is one of many I'm sure. Those hoity toity owners talk and know all about each other. They don't give a tinker's damn about us as long as we lay low. All they want to do is rake in their money, their profits."

Ben almost said that his soon-to-be brother in law was a Cripple Creek mine owner. Him and his sister, Abby. Ben was flooded with longing for Abby. And with images of her as she begged him not to get on the train that summer day. She had been, and Ben hoped still was, his girl.

He thought of Lon, Abby and the Double I. Those two sure as heck didn't rake money in. The mine income was not huge. It was a good amount. But to keep track of it, they would need a whisk broom not a rake. But he didn't care about all that right now. He just kind of shrugged while Cow went on.

"Our real worry is that horse's patoot Pinkerton and his men. They are the ones hired by the owners to dog us. Those guys would love to hunt us down. You, me, and any other miner shoved out of town for not disowning the union. You know they'll at least keep eyes out. They're watching for men like us—miners who are on someone's blacklist. They probably hope we will come around, somewhere near a mining camp. So they can jump us. You wait and see, they'll be there."

He spat again, angrily. "I hope they all rot on the seventh level of hell."

Ben chuckled, not amused. "Tell me about it. I think that farm woman, Mrs. Cobbson, had it right. We need to choose what we do now. Too bad the options aren't clear." He paused, wondering about the future—somehow go back to mining, get into something around the ranch business, or what?

He went on. "Hamlin gets us put on a train. The engineer dumps us off just over the state line. With nothing but what was in our pockets. We try to look for work. Locals hate and fear us. The owners talk to each other. They know us. Won't hire us. Won't let us find work in the mines. Those fat cats take it easy, easy for them but not us. I agree, our real worry is those damn pinks. Those sons of bitches would as soon kill as look at us."

Tossing a piece of wood on the campfire, Ben thought back. What a strange few weeks!

He and Cow didn't know each other before the train. They had buddied up on the ride out of Cripple. That way at least they each had someone to rely on, watch their back, to commiserate with.

Both wanted to get back to their loved ones but that wasn't easy. Having a target on their back didn't add anything good.

And the pinks, employees of the Pinkerton and other 'security' agencies didn't help. Those guys dogging them sure made for deep waters. Those hired thugs wanted to run union men out of the country. Most of them were acting for the owners, sure. But many of them liked to chase and beat union men just for the fun of it.

Cow coughed. "I try to think what I could have done different not to get put on that train."

Ben nodded. "Me too. But I just wanted a living wage. And to be paid for the work I actually did. That shouldn't get you run out of town, out of work. I've thought long and hard on that, and I have to say that I'd do it again."

The fire was dying. Cow stared into the dancing reds and blacks and shimmering energy. Not Ben. He yawned, stretched. "Me, I'm gonna get some sleep. Going to roll up in this blanket I bought down in Raton. G'night!"

The stars shone on, answering no questions, giving no comfort.

I

THE TIP OF THE BAYONET STEERED BEN RIGHT INTO THE RAIL car. The militiaman pulled back, stepped down and away. It was a horse transport car, not a passenger wagon. He turned to protest but the door rolled shut, creaking then latching from the outside. It sounded ominous, certainly not announcing a pleasure run.

The train lurched, moved. He looked around the car at twenty five or more miners. Their faces radiated fear, dejection, anger, denial. Three over in a corner were noisily playing cards. Some looked spellbound, staring ahead but not seeing, trying to make sense of the moment. He kind of recognized a few of them.

A grateful thought ran through his mind: Good thing it was June. At least they likely wouldn't have a snow storm. He squeezed between others sitting on the floor of the cattle car, sat and leaned back, tried to rest. And he noticed that they had at least swept and hosed out the car before packing miners in. Spotless it was not. But there were no road apples, no turds or mounds of hay. Still, the car stunk of manure, horse piss, and sweating miners.

At that he laughed, a chuckle then a roar. This day was all a bunch of shit, horse or bull, whatever.

A voice broke through. "What's so funny?"

"Better to laugh than cry, right? At least that's the saying."

The voice ignored Ben's reply and droned on.

"Dammit all. We're getting shoved, literally railroaded out of town. For no reason. We didn't do anything but try to improve our workplace. I'm not sure my wife even knows what's happening to me. How can you laugh?"

Ben just looked at him, then laughed again.

The man sat next to Ben, leaning on the wall. He seemed tallish, and not too stocky. There was a hint of an accent.

"I for one am furious. This is outrageous! Not funny at all."

Ben figured the accent was somewhere east coast, or old world, or something. Not sure.

Watching, alert and hoping that he could handle him, Ben was silent, watching to see if the guy got aggressive. Unlikely, but who knows, he thought.

Taking a breath, he blurted.

"I was just thinking. This is a horse transporter—this car. But at least there is no manure here, at least I don't see or feel any. But actually we're all just about drowning in shit. It may as well be this deep." At that he held his hand flat up just at his upper lip.

A few of the miners, now ex miners he guessed, glance his way. Some saw his gesture and heard him. A sprinkle of them chuckled halfheartedly. No one roared; one or two smiled weakly.

The tallish man looked around and grinned sourly. He seemed to weigh matters, make a decision. Abruptly out came his hand, ready to shake not hit.

"My name is Cow, or I should say that is what I answer to. Born Carlton Orville Weston. The third." He said this in a singsong rhythm. "Schoolkids called me Cow and worse, but Cow stuck."

They shook. "I'm Ben. Ben McNall. Benjamin Franklin McNall—my parents believed in naming us kids for famous people. Hoping it rubbed off. My brother is George Armstrong Custer McNall, and so on."

"George Armstrong Custer, huh? I hope his luck doesn't rub off on your brother. I'll take my luck with Cow, thanks. It's a moo-ving experience!"

Ben groaned, glad for the levity.

Cow continued. "Anyway, nice to meet you Ben. I guess."

He apologetically glanced for having said that. "You know what I mean, not excited about being here. No insult intended."

"None taken. I've already had my fill of insult and injury today."

Looking around, Cow sniffed and groaned. "Do you have any idea where we're headed?"

The train lurched onto a siding, stopped. They heard the engine of another makeup pass by, heading north up towards Cripple.

"No. The tour guide was out so I didn't get a brochure. They were in a hurry for me to board so nobody filled me in." Ben grinned, tried to laugh. "Maybe there'll be tea and cakes for us down the road when we stop."

Cow ignored the humor, scrunching in, trying to get comfortable, and seemed to drop off to sleep.

Ben wasn't sure what to make of the guy. Talkative as a parrot one minute, withdrawn and sleepy the next. He hoped the guy was just stressed, not unstable. All in all, he was an odd exclamation mark to a very memorable and unpleasant day!

It was dark and they had been riding for hours that seemed like weeks. The cars creaked, coasting and slowing. Ben shook his head, elbowed the man Cow. "We're here, wherever that is. Be ready for anything."

Brakes squeaked. They groaned to a stop. The door noisily slid open. A militia man filled the opening, bayonet at the ready, yelling obscenities. He stepped down, keeping his weapon visible, shaking and thrusting it menacingly.

"End of tracks, maggots! Get yer butts up off the floor and get out! Out! Move it, move it, move it!"

As the men piled out someone asked, "Where are we?"

Ben thought, 'At the state line. Probably Kansas or New Mexico, or maybe Wyoming.'

The soldier grinned and spat.

"I told ya. Your ride is over. Out!" He shrugged, added a nugget of truth. "You are in northern New Mexico. Just past the Colorado state line." His wicked grin flashed again. "Have fun, maggots!"

The militiaman checked the car to be sure it was empty. Another soldier, also with rifle and bayonet, kept watch on the miners. "Move back you men. Get back!"

The first grabbed the handle and pulled the door shut. Other uniformed teams up and down the train did pretty much the same. Then the uniformed mob climbed into a passenger car. "Good luck, suckers!"

Ben and Cow watched as the train backed away. Ben clasped his arms close and gave thanks that Abby, this morning, insisted he put on a long sleeved shirt.

"At least the weather is with us—no rain or wind."

Cow jumped up and down, from cold or nerves, Ben wasn't sure. "Yup, not yet anyway. Now what?"

Ben looked around, found the Big Dipper and the North Star.

"Now we walk. Raton should be over that way." Pointing.

Cow. "You sure, man?"

"No. I'm not, not absolutely. But I'm sure not going to stand here and wait for someone to come around."

He looked at the tallish, suddenly insecure man. "Cow, isn't it? C'mon Cow. Time to hoof it. So to speak." He couldn't help but laugh. After a moment Cow did too.

Ben turned towards Raton and stepped out, not even looking look back. If he had to go alone, so be it. There was certainly no reason to wait. Either nothing would happen. That or the wolves would circle, literally or figuratively. No way was he going to hang around for that.

Cow was right behind. Others followed as well. Shortly, conversation started.

"I can find my way around a mine any time, with a candle or without. But put me out here outdoors in the forest... I'm a babe in the woods. How in hell do you know where to head, Ben?" Cow looked intently.

Ben pointed up. "North Star. Keep that over your right shoulder and you're heading west."

"Oh. I'm not sure which is the North Star, but I believe you." He grinned. "I'll stick with you."

The grin disappeared and his shoulders slumped. "Boy, I sure miss my wife and kids. Gotta get word to them somehow. I don't think they know what happened to me."

That made Ben think of Abby. Did she have any idea where he was? Whether he was even alive? Suddenly he wondered if he had done the right thing. Maybe he should have stayed in Cripple and taken the manager job. He could have married Abby and become a mine owner. Life on easy street...

The sound of a dog barking brought him back. No. Miners weren't dogs to be fed and used and kicked. He was sure he made the right decision. To climb aboard and be deported.

He shrugged, reassuring his new friend. "There'll be a telegraph, maybe even a telephone exchange."

Cow looked skeptically over. "A telephone exchange! My! Aren't we hoity toity—who has a telephone anyway? I got away with a few nickels so maybe I can afford to send a short 'gram. Say, is that the glow of the town? Raton?"

Just as he said this, a figure loomed in the dark. It was another man with a rifle. And a few more back behind. They held their weapons at port arms, ready to be used in a flash. The miners cautiously stopped, those in back bumping into Cow and Ben. As they neared a sheriff's star on his chest stood out.

Harshly, "Where you boys from?"

Someone blurted, "Victor. That is, Cripple Creek."

The sheriff grabbed his hat and hit it on his thigh in anger. The one handed rifle pointed up for which Ben was glad. Any flying bullet would go harmlessly away.

"More miners from Cripple? Hell, how many of you this time?"

Hat back on, he looked them over. More than one miner felt like a lamb being ogled by a coyote.

"Well, men. We don't really want you. You can pass through, that's all. The mayor says we will put you up for a night. In the town park. The Ladies Aid of one of the churches has blankets and some food. But after one night you need to move on quick as you can. The park is straight ahead two blocks."

He pointed. "I mean it, we don't want you. One night, then move on. We arrest vagrants here. And put 'em to work—no free room and board."

Staring at the miners, the lawman looked each of the men in the eye. Ben watched as he worked to memorize each face. Abruptly he turned and motioned. "Come on, men." He and his posse strode away.

One of the miners spat. "Vagrant hell. Yesterday I was a working man. Today I'm thrown out of a job and run out of town with nothing but my shirt. What am I supposed to do?" Some of the miners muttered in agreement.

Ben shrugged. "Me, I'm going to eat something then wrap up in a Ladies Aid blanket for a few hours."

Cow was already a few steps ahead.

II

As a kid Ben and his brothers would sometimes take a blanket out and sleep in the orchard or a field. It was fun. Not so this time. Night in the park, wrapped in a blanket on the ground, seemed to last twice as long as the train ride. At least that was how his back felt when an empty stomach and birds chirping woke him up. He slowly, sorely stood. It took a moment's look around to remember where and why he was there. He kind of smiled as he lightly booted Cow.

"Let's go find the telegraph office."

It wasn't hard to find the Western Union shop. The operator looked him over like he was a fish several days on the beach. "You a Colorado miner? Can't give no credit. Cash on the barrel head, a nickel a word."

"A nickel! That is over five times what it cost me last week to send one!"

"Yeah, well, this ain't last week. We're overrun with you bums. Pay up or git." He scowled and pointedly glanced at his .45 revolver on the table, close to hand.

Ben coldly sneered and turned to go. Cow, just behind him, grabbed his arm.

"I have money."

"Oh? You're not just another penniless grasping miner? Out to take Raton to the devil?"

Cow mumbled so softly Ben had to lean in to hear. "I managed to fill my pockets before they poked my behind onto the train."

"So, more than a few nickels, huh?"

"Yup." He grinned as they stepped out of line. Ben threw one more look at the operator. That man ignored it and was already berating the next miner in line.

"Ben, you can give me your message. I'll have my wife pass it on. Or better, I'll front you a buck."

One buck means I can say twenty words, Ben thought. "That's fine of you, Cow. Are you sure? I'll repay as soon as I can."

Cow rubbed his stomach. "Whenever you can is fine with me. No rush. First let's go find a real meal. Telegrams can wait an hour. Don't know about you, but last night's Ladies Aid soup and crackers were welcome but they sure didn't stick. Right now I'm starved. My treat."

Filling the stomach was the first positive thing in two days or so. Concentrating on a stack of pancakes was way better than fretting and worrying.

Soon the yawning hole their lives were in came back to attention, front and center.

"Thanks, Cow. Nothing like a full stomach to help face the day." Ben reminded himself to update Cow's IOU. He added 65 cents for the hot cakes and coffee to the dollar for the telegram. He would repay somehow some time.

Cow splayed his hands as if throwing dust up so gold would settle out, or something. Ben took it to mean 'what the heck'.

"Well, Ben, I feel better. Agreed, full stomach and all. Now, we need to figure out what to do. Where to go. How to get there. How to spot and avoid pinks. How to get cleaned up, fed, clothed. Other than that, hey, it will be a slow and easy day, no?"

"Pinks. Yeah. I forgot about pinks with the train ride and hike and all. Those damn Pinkerton agents will be looking for us deported miners."

He glanced around the room, seeing no obvious ex cops or thugs, and went on.

"Those bums will do their best to keep us from a mine job. Probably will work to keep us away from the mining camps altogether. Or, more likely, let us come near then jump us."

"Yup." For a minute or so they concentrated on emptying their plates.

"You know, Cow, maybe we should change names. Their lists will show Cow Weston and Ben McNall. I'm thinking of using another name, maybe Frank Mack. What about you?"

Cow noisily slurped his coffee. Ben hated that sound. As a kid he remembered his mother giving a slap if he did it. Small problem, he decided, and tried not to react. Cow considered a name change, deep in thought then spoke suddenly.

"Nah. Most or probably all of them don't know us by sight. A few could I guess, but not enough to worry. Hell, they have hundreds of people to watch for. And a few miners just might get after them, so they'll be wary and not crowd us."

Another slurp.

"Anyway, Ben, those goons will just have a list of names. The thing to do is keep our heads down and hats up. And be careful about putting names on passenger lists or anywhere a pink could see it. Not that they can read, but still… How about you be Frank Mack and something like Orv Tyson for me?"

Ben nodded. "You're right. If we need to give a name to the conductor or someone, it can be something like that, changing every ride. But you're right. May as well just live out in the open—carefully—as much as we can. Still, we need to keep our eyes out for pinks."

Cow smirked. "Heck, like I say, half of those thugs probly can't read anyway."

"Yup, no point being a target." Ben chuckled. "The first thing we need to do, Cow, is let the homefolk know."

"Yup. Let's go send a few telegrams."

There was no line so they took a seat on a park bench. Deciding what to say to their loved one wasn't as easy as they had thought.

Cow's generosity floored Ben and he would remember it always. A dollar at five cents a word meant twenty words at most. He knew what he wanted to say, how to word it was the thing.

He wanted to say he was alright and in Raton; please send money care of Stockmens bank here; my new public name is Frank Mack; and to let her know it was really him. To do that, he decided, he'd ask about the Double I. Maybe she could meet him in Pueblo after the school year. He kind of ran out of words, both the number for the telegram and how to say that, so he just signed off.

The operator gruffly but willingly took Cow's money and promptly sent two telegrams.

IN CRIPPLE CREEK, THINGS HAD SETTLED DOWN. NO MORE pitched battles of miners and 'security' men. No more dynamite explosions. The Militia hadn't gone home but were easing up a bit. At least they weren't prodding men with their bayonets. And no longer were they forbidding three or more people from talking in public. They weren't out day and night patrolling the streets, a least not regularly.

The Western Federation of Miners, the union which caused all the uproar, was out of business. At least in Cripple Creek it was—the miners were all deported to New Mexico or Kansas. Union owned stores had been looted. There was no more trouble making by union members—no more random shots fired, no trains derailed, no beatings doled out in alleys. Big Bill Haywood, President, hadn't shown his face in Cripple. Rumor had it he was in Denver then headed to New York City.

Townsfolk and miners went on about their business, picking up pieces and repairing damaged property. Gold came out of the ground steadily. Owners and investors were happy.

Abby Bosini wearily plodded home after one of the last days of the school year. She loved teaching but sometimes didn't like school. A boy named Nate stood at her door. She knew him because he had been in her class but had stopped coming. Nate smiled and glanced at the envelope in hand.

"Miss Bosini, hello! I have a telegram for you." He held out one hand, the 'gram in the other.

She gave him a penny and took the envelope. "I miss you in class, Nate. I hope you come back next year."

"Nah, I won't be back to play with pencils and look at books. I can make real money doing this! Thanks!" He pocketed the tip, gave a mock salute, and trotted off.

Abby went in, closed the door and tore it open, dreading but also eager. It was short and condensed like all telegrams:

AM WELL RATON stop HOW YOU HOLDING UP stop SEND MONEY FRANK MACK AT STOCKMENS BANK stop HOW DOUBLE I stop YOUR DEPORTEE stop

About twenty little words. She sat. Sobbed a bit with relief. Gazing at nothing and thinking, she lost track of time.

Brother Lon opened the door slowly and painfully. Not that long ago he had been shot in Victor. Several others got it too during the chaos at a town gathering just after a big explosion. The Mine Owners Association had called a meeting in Victor. Things went south and several people got injured, Lon among them. His wound was healing and he didn't want to pull on it. Getting shot in the labor fights made him reevaluate. He paid more attention to those around him. He realized there was more to life than following a vein and reading assay reports.

He saw that his sister seemed pensive as she glanced up and handed him the telegram.

"Ben is in Raton, in New Mexico. He is alright!"

He scanned the paper, smiling. "Good to hear he is safe. Or at least alright. Send money, huh? Who is Frank Mack— maybe an officer at that bank?" He thought a moment. "At least we know it is him. Who else knows about the Double I?"

The Double I was a reasonably profitable mine. He and Abby owned it there in Cripple Creek. The name honored their heritage: One parent was Irish and the other Italian. Lon was fair and blond while she had dark hair and an olive complexion. Rarely tagged as siblings, they occasionally used that confusion to advantage.

He set the 'gram down, then himself.

"So, now what?"

"I'll send some money and help him get back."

"Back? He can't come here, Ab."

She glared. He felt for her but he had to say why.

"Remember this is a guy who was run out of town at bayonet point. As of today in this mining camp he couldn't get a job sweeping the streets much less as a miner. Guys like him who show up won't be welcomed. They'll be beaten then bundled out of the camp. Or worse."

He shrugged, gently clasped her shoulder with his good hand. "Ben McNall cannot show his face here in Cripple."

She crumbled, fighting back tears, voice quavering. "I'm afraid you are right, Lon. He'll have to go somewhere else. Probably stay out of mining."

She looked around as if hoping to find something positive. "No mining for a while, at least gold and silver. Aren't there coal mines up north, Boulder, and over by Trinidad?"

He smiled. "He knows the score. That's why Frank Mack—he won't put his name out in public. At least not now. I'm glad he's being cautious."

She stood. "I'll send some money to Stockmens Bank in Raton. To Mr. Mack, and you are probably right. Ben is just being careful."

BACK IN RATON, THE TWO MEN TALKED. OR AT LEAST COW DID.

"Alright. At least now someone knows where we are. I know my wife will be glad to hear from me. We should now start to get some help and support, I hope. But today, here in Raton we need to avoid the sheriff. Him, I don't want to tangle with right now."

Ben nodded, his eyes on a man who was circulating. A tad alarmed, more irritated, his eyes followed the guy around. He was dressed like a farmer but his face was not sunburnt. He walked and talked with assurance. The 'farmer' was going around and chatting up some of the miners in the park.

"Look Cow. I think that man is a goon, a pink. Or he's a businessman being awful friendly. Come on, let's see what his game is." They walked over towards the man who looked him and Cow up and down.

He smiled frostily. "You're miners, ex-miners that is. And you're new in town trying to figure out what's happening, I can tell. Relax. I'm not a goon or a Pinkerton. I mean youall no harm."

He extended his hand. "I'm Jerome Cobbson."

Ben put on his own glacial smile, nodded, shook the hand. "You're sure talking to a lot of folks. Making a list are you?"

"Matter of fact I am. A list of possible workers for my farm. My wife and I need help, farm help. Can you cut and pitch hay? Feed horses? Hoe weeds? If you can, and you will, we can deal."

He waited silently. Then went on.

"We'll provide three squares a day and let you sleep in the hay loft. All the clean water you can drink. No liquor allowed. Two dollars a day, cash, paid after dinnertime. Interested?"

Cow nodded minutely as Ben glanced over. His smile didn't widen but it did soften a bit.

"I'm Frank. Yes, I can do that. And I'm interested."

Cow stepped forward. "And I'm Orv, with him. When do we start?

III

HAYING WAS HARD. BEN WAS REMINDED HOW IT WAS HARD, sweaty work. And how it made him ache. Mucking ore in a mine was no picnic. Still, it seemed easier and more rewarding than moving hay or shoveling horse manure out of a barn stall. Ben had forgotten—on purpose—how he detested the hard and unrelenting days on his parent's farm. He remembered again why he had lit out for the west's mining towns.

He shook his head and smiled ruefully. When he left the family farm he swore he would never again sling hay. Yet here he was with a pitchfork in a hayfield ablaze with sun. The dust on his forehead turned to mud and ran into his eyes. Wiping with his shirttail and the back of his hand kind of cleared his vision.

The farmer snorted, "Hey, rock man. Stop grinning and get that fork a-lifting! This ain't a mine. Maybe you can get away with slow moving ore, but not my hay!

He watched as Ben stuck the pitchfork under a heap of dried alfalfa and grass. He braced the handle against his thigh, ready to move the load. 'I forgot this stuff could be so heavy' was all Ben could think. With a groan he rested his hand with the fork on the leg, pushing with his thigh and back to start the motion. With that momentum he levered the fork up and managed to get most of the hay onto the waiting wagon.

Cobbson knew that only with practice could a person move hay that way. He was impressed and almost asked how long Ben had worked a farm. Instead he made as if to sneer, not show approval. He knew these miners could get cocky. There were a lot of them around and most of them hungry. Others could be hired easily. No need to be a nice guy.

"Not bad for a rock slug. Next time try to get it all on the wagon, not just half." He pointed at another heap eight or ten feet away. "You too!" This at Cow who stood by another heap.

Next try, Ben got it all onto the wagon, and couldn't resist smiling. Unwittingly he muttered. At the farmer but half to himself, he spoke.

"This really is kind of like mucking ore down in the mine." Mucking was a basic chore. Everyone did it from time to time and the new hires full time. It was simply moving— by shovel or by hand—rocks from the blasted face to an ore car for transport for refining. Big and small pieces, in the tunnel. He continued. "With this hay at least I am earning cash and get some good meals, to boot."

"Yeah, well, there's more." Cobbson wasn't sure if this was sass or honest conversation. He pointed at a whole line of little hay piles. "Get those piles up on the wagon and then we'll break for dinner."

Ben grew up in the Midwest where people ate breakfast, dinner at noon, and supper in the evening. In the mines it was breakfast, lunch, dinner at end of day. Here today at Cobbson's farm, mid-day dinner it was.

As he forked hay he thought, 'Man, I haven't called the noon meal that in quite a while.' Images of his mother and sister cooking and serving heaping plates jumped to mind. 'I forget about being on a midwesterner's place. Call the meal what you will, I can't wait—I am starving.'

An older woman, probably the farmer's wife, stood at the table. It was set with plates, knives and forks. Cow, Ben, and the others rinsed hands and face in a rain barrel before sitting.

"Here's chicken and taters and beans and bread and coffee. Help yourself and pass it on. Water in that keg." She pointed to a keg with a spout. "There's more of everything so fill yourselves up. You still have a lot of hay to move."

Cow and Ben ate then went out and moved hay for another five or six hours. They stopped by the house for water and to be paid before walking to town. They had earlier agreed to spend another night in town, hopefully a hotel if the money came through. If not, the park bench. Neither wanted to stay and sleep in the hay loft.

"Mr. Cobbson tells me you are Cripple Creek Miners. You got in trouble with the owners I hear."

"Yes ma'am. Four days ago we were miners, now we're refugees."

"Well, you two men, you be on watch for Pinkerton goons. They are all over Raton, looking to make trouble with the likes of you. As if you don't have enough already."

Ben took a chance. "Mrs. Cobbson, that's you, right? Thank you ma'am for the good meal, and the advice. We have seen a few pinks already and want nothing to do with them. We're just trying to figure out where to go from here, what to do. Go back to mining, find another job, not sure."

She looked appraisingly at them. "Well, you have a choice to make. Go back to mining, you'll likely be chased by goons the rest of your life. Or you can find a new line of work."

Smiling, she turned to look at the kitchen area. "Why, I know some young women who would love to meet up with men to start a farm or store." Smilingly, "And a family."

Ben filled a ladle from the keg and drank. Cow smiled. "Thanks but we're both taken."

She nodded. "Either way, you have a choice to make. Think hard on it."

WALKING BACK TO RATON FROM THE RANCH, THEY KEPT THEIR own tired thoughts. As they neared town, Cow broke the silence.

"I hope my wife sent the money today. This two bucks Mr. Farmer—what is his name, Cobbson? Anyway, what he pays us field hands won't go far. Even with a good midday meal. And I sure don't want to move hay for the rest of my life. Or even one more day if I can avoid it!"

Ben smiled. "Agreed, hopefully not another day. I'll take mine work anytime over field work. Let's swing by and see. I asked for the money sent to Stockmens Bank. How about you?"

Cow snorted. The sound made Ben laugh. Cow looked hurt. "Not me. I asked for it sent to New Mexico State Bank. Meet there in half an hour?"

"Alright. See you..." Just then Ben caught a man staring. The wise farm wife's warning of goons came to mind. The guy was in a dark suit. And he was visibly armed. No sheriff's star or anything. The guy fit in like a man barefoot in church. And he was not trying to hide his evil eyed gaze. Ben looked on past him, appearing to ignore it all. Coolly and softly he spoke.

"Don't look now, but there's a pink or some other goon over there. Eying us. Yeah, let's go get our money. And then get out of this viper's nest."

"Sure, Ben. It is time. See you at the State Bank in little bit."

At Stockmens Bank the clerk looked him over. "So you are Frank Mack are you?" His glare made Ben wonder what response he wanted.

"Well the sender wants me to ask you a question or two. Tell me, who owns these mines, up in Cripple Creek? The Corkscrew and the Double I. In Cripple Creek." He sat back, placidly waiting. The sender had paid a buck to have the question asked.

"I do not know the Corkscrew, couldn't tell you whose it is. The Double I, now that one I do. It is owned by Dillon Bosini and Abigail Bosini, Lon and Abby."

The man almost looked disappointed. Then he nodded, counting out bills.

"Your sender asked for that answer. Here is your one hundred dollars, Mr. Mack." He flicked at a form, a receipt, not even looking. "Sign here."

Ben scrawled something on the form, then sent a quick telegram.

Funds received thanks stop What is corkscrew stop Am headed yr way will be in touch stop Your deportee

As he left Cow came in. "I have to let her know. Give me a few minutes."

THE TWO SAT ON A PARK BENCH.

"Like you said, that's enough pitching hay. Time to move on." Ben scanned the plaza and around. No besuited security men were to be seen. He looked over.

"Cow my man, what do we do next? Maybe go take a look at some other mine towns? Creede, Crested Butte, Bonanza, I even hear there is an iron ore mine up past Saguache. What do you think?"

"I don't know." Cow too looked around for eavesdroppers; was relieved to see none.

"You know, the owners will be on the lookout at mining towns. You just saw some Pinkerton suit lurking around the station here. Near mining camps, they'll be thick as flies at a butchering. One of the guys on the train said he was heading back to Cripple. More than one of the others told him don't do it. They'll kill you."

He frowned. "And Ben, I am afraid those guys are right. This is no time to be a hero."

"I imagine so." The eyes of the guy that morning almost made Ben shiver. Then the whole thing made him mad. "Those security bastards have never done an honest day's work. They'd be helpless as a puppy in a mine. Too bad we can't..."

Cow smiled and interrupted. "And I heard a tunnel is being bored from the river to the Montrose area. Gunnison River. For an irrigation project. They are advertising for hard rock men to do the job. Maybe there are jobs with railroads or other irrigation projects are out there. Not just the Montrose area, but out and around." He gestured, waving a hand.

NEITHER SPOKE FOR A WHILE.

Ben sighed. "I really don't know much else. Besides mining, I mean."

Cow smiled again. "You mean you don't want to go back to farming? The food was good but you don't like moving hay by the pitchfork?"

Ben punched his shoulder lightly. "Not only no but hell no. I ran from the farm as a kid for good reason. This reminded me all about it."

Cow nodded. "Hey, I grew up in the city. One day was more than enough to make me swear off farm work forever. I'd rather run sheep or manage a dog kennel."

Ben grinned. "Seriously, I think we ought to at least poke our noses into some of those places. Mining towns. Quiet like and very carefully. Just a quick in and out to see how bad, or good, things are. You know, Frank and Orv are just guys looking to see what is happening. Maybe we're seeing ghosts, and they'll hire us on. Then we can get on with things. Reunite with family and loved ones…"

MISTER COBBSON RODE INTO THE PLAZA. GOT OFF AND TIED up his horse. He looked around and spotted his quarry.

"Oh jeez. There's our farmer, Ben. Cobbson. And he's walking this way."

"Well, I don't want to move hay again. We'll tell him no, agreed?"

He smiled, hostile like, at the farmer. "Hell no we won't return our pay. We worked hard for it!"

The man chuckled. "You earned it, I agree. I'm not here to quibble. But I am glad to find you."

Ben smirked. "Here we are."

Cobbson stopped, apparently ready to chat. "Did you think I'd just let good workers go away?"

He held up his hands, showing he came in peace.

"Hear me out. No haystacks or pitch forks for you, alright?" He looked each of them in the eye.

"You guys proved good workers who don't need babied. Men who can think for themselves."

"Glad you recognize talent."

"No need to be sarcastic. The thing is, I have a proposition for you."

Cow glanced at Ben who shrugged.

"Let me ask you this. Can you manage a horse? I know you are miners, but can you stay in the saddle at a trot and pull the reins?"

Both men nodded but said nothing, waiting to hear his offer.

Cobbson nodded to himself as well. "So. Horse riding you can do. Well, besides the farm I have cattle. The hay you forked up yesterday is for them in the winter. I need them—the cattle—brought in."

Stopping to look the men in the eye, he went on. "Will pay you the two dollars a day for the next two or three, however long it takes. Deal?"

Cow glanced at Ben, smiled. "You provide the grub, and a bottle of whiskey, and pay us each four a day and we're on."

"Four?! Hell, maybe I should sign over my firstborn too. Two and a half. And grub."

Ben murmured just loud enough. "Do I hear five?"

The man held up hands again in surrender. "Alright. Alright. I'll go four. Four dollars a day per man. Horses provided, with grub and drink, and a little bag of oats for the horse. Start now."

They stood and shook on the agreement.

"Mister Cobbson. What should we call you? I go by Ben." Gesturing he grinned. "And, no joke, this guy goes by Cow."

Cobbson noticed the new names but asked not. He just nodded. In a frontier railroad town, the less questions asked the less one had to pretend not to know. He simply took it in.

""Ben, Cow, welcome aboard. Call me Ed. So Ben, make sure you round up only the four legged cows. Don't bring this varmint to me!" He too grinned.

"Seriously, men. Let's go talk but let me see to the horse." He headed for his mount, took its reins, retied them to a hitching post.

"Lets get coffee." Leading them to a café, they sat and ordered. No talk went on as they waited to be served.

Cobbson sipped, smiled. "This joe is excellent. Mrs Cobbson and I get along well, but her coffee could be used to tan leather. Should be." He made a show of looking around. "Don't tell her I said that!"

"Said what?" Cow asked.

Cobbson nodded and got to business.

"The reason I am hiring you is serious. There are gangs out nabbing calves and their mamas. Not just a few of mine, but many." He got a piece of paper out and spread it on the table.

"This here is my ranch's brand. See, it is the 'Bar C'.

They looked at a capital C with a bar under it: C̲

Cobbson refolded the paper. "What is going on is, these guys will find a mama with our brand. If they do, then they change her brand. Maybe put a bar on top, or add a slant or something. And put the same on any unbranded calfs or others they find. Then the cows look legitimate for them to send to market."

Ben frowned. "Sounds like outright theft to me."

"You damn right it is. And if you catch them in the act, great. Don't get yourself shot; if need be let them go but get word to me. If you can, then hogtie 'em and bring em in. Either way, we'll be glad to take care of them."

Cow glanced over; Ben shrugged. Neither really wanted to know what that meant.

Ben wondered. "So you want us to be detectives and be our own posse. If we catch some yayhoos playing games with your cattle, which do you want? If we can't deliver everything, which should we do? Bring in the cattle or the rustlers?"

IV

Cow yipped at the question. For some reason the sound made Ben grin.

"Ain't funny Ben. Those guys will be armed I'm sure. No way do I want to go up against armed thieves doing a job. With just my good intentions."

Cobbson thought a moment. "Yeah, like I said, don't get yourself shot. These guys are outlaws, or cowboys out on the edge of the law. And they are sure as hell carrying. Be careful. Tell you what. I'll get you each a .45 pistol and a shotgun. With ammo. And dock you a dollar a day until they are paid for." He stood.

"Deal? Be at the ranch out where you forked hay today. Seven tomorrow morning. Be ready to go, to be gone for four or so days. I'll pay you for half a day today. Matter of fact, here."

He took out a five dollar bill and handed it Cow. Smiling, he turned to leave. "See you then."

Ben stood, watched Cobbson ride off.

"I don't know, Cow. This smells."

Cow looked at the fiver, smiling. He ignored Ben who went on.

"Maybe we're better off dodging pinks. At least we can recognize one and know what to do next."

He shrugged. "This just seems odd. The man didn't answer my question. Are we deputized lawmen or approved hired hands, bringing in rustlers? Or are we cowpokes retrieving unbranded or misbranded cattle?"

Ben's eyes widened. "For that matter if we find some of his stock, what's to stop the sheriff from accusing us of rustling? And jailing us. Or stringing us up? And why did this supposedly frugal farmer guy pay us several dollars each to do nothing for the rest of today?"

He sat back down, arms crossed defensively. "I think we are in over our heads here, friend."

"Jeez!" Cow shook his head. "That makes my head spin. Good money. But, if we do stumble on some rustlers they won't take it kindly. Those guys are armed. And touchy—likely they shoot first and ask questions if anyone survives."

Cow rubbed his temples, frowning. "The more we talk, the better your plan to go find mine work sounds. At least good paying ore doesn't double cross ya!"

His face split with an evil, enthusiastic grin. "Double cross, what a phrase. Anyway, Ben, here's an idea. Let's show up tomorrow ready to go. Get the horses and guns. And the grub and whiskey. We go out for a week. This is big country, know what I mean? We likely will see no one, nothing. Come back, get paid for trying, and play it from there."

Ben thought on it, smiled. "Yeah. I agree, we should go out. Make a show of best efforts and all. But, funny thing, we can't find anything. We see nothing. We ride around like he told us to but see no one, no cattle or calves. Maybe that happens for a few weeks before we pool some money to get back home. Or at some point he fires us because we're not cut out for the job."

Cow pulled out the fiver. "Let's spend this on a hotel. Don't know about you, but I'd rather not spend another night on a park bench. Looks like we may be on the trail for a while after today."

Sleeping in a bed after cleaning up felt darn good. Morning came soon, and a meal.

Cow slurped some water and spoke excitedly through a mouthful of bacon and eggs. "Alright Deputy Ben, let's get a move on. Cobbson awaits."

Ben swallowed the last of his coffee. "Yer right, Sheriff Cow. Time to move." They left and strode to the farm.

The sun was just over the horizon, promising a clear and warm day. Ben had hoped for a few clouds.

They saddled up and mounted quietly. They didn't have to wait long for word from the boss man.

Cobbson swung his arm in a big arc. "We've usually run our herds on the range to the north and west. Our cattle are grazing out there now. So that is where I want you to concentrate. Of course the bad guys will be out there somewhere too. With their branding irons. Go get 'em!"

The rancher slapped the near horse on the flank and grinned as it leaped forward. Ben expected it. His guard was up so he sat tall. He stayed on easily and slowed the animal until Cow caught up.

At first they rode apart, wary and alert. Soon that stopped and they simply headed north and west, casually looking around, chatting just a bit. No effort was made at stealth nor did they try to make noise or raise dust. They didn't go out of their way to look into obvious hiding spots.

"Hey, it is about four o'clock. Whaddya say, let's find a camp spot. I need some food and coffee. This riding quiet like and spooking around gets old."

"Yea, I agree Cow, this is almost as tiresome as farm work. A small fire between rocks won't show much, and I need some coffee too."

After dark they let the fire die down. Ben watched the mesmerizing glow of the coals, dancing red, orange, black, blue and green with fingers of flame from time to time.

"You know," he drawled, "I still don't see why Cobbson is paying us so much. Twice a day's farm pay to come out and look for his cattle? Which he should have experienced crews doing full time? There is something else going on here."

Cow sipped on a coffee cup half full of Cobbson's whiskey.

"Whew, that is some rotgut stuff. Tastes like he got mud puddle water for his distillery setup. Probably this is a brand new batch, just out of the kettle. I doubt aging would improve it. Ah well. Down the hatch with Raton Lightning!" He tossed the cup back, coughed, then responded.

Ben laughed. "So we don't even rate hooch from Taos!?"

Cow nodded. "Hey we're the new guys. Don't knock it!" He made sure to get the last sip.

"I agree with you, pardner. Cobbson's hiring us don't make sense. You know, maybe he wants to be able to say he had someone out looking, guarding his herds. But if he's up to something…"

He poured another cupful of hooch but didn't drink, just looked at it.

"Maybe he's working both sides of the street. Has us out supposedly patrolling where he says pickings ought to be good. And he tells his other men where he sent us. So they do their rustling undisturbed. If asked, he can he can truthfully say he has crews out looking for bad guys."

"God, I hope not. I want no part of cattle trafficking, even if we are supposed to be the good guys. I'd rather dodge pinks."

The second day they didn't keep distance. Riding side by side, they talked little. They expected and saw only an occasional coyote or deer. No people or cattle.

Day three they just rode and talked. That evening they again started a small fire. After all no smoke would be visible after dark. The glow was minimal since they kept the flames low and set between two big rocks.

"Man, this poking into each valley and pasture, pretending to look, is boring as all get out." Ben tossed a small twig onto the flames.

Cow chuckled. "Three days and I'm almost hoping to see a cow or a cowpoke. At least the weather has held fair."

"Yeah. I really thought we'd see an old campfire ring or tracks or something. But we're hip deep in quiet and solitude."

Cow burped. "Ooh, that Raton Lightning! But like I said the other day, I think maybe Cobbson is working both sides of the street. He doesn't expect us to see many cows or calves. Probably no sheep either."

He rolled up in a blanket. "Yup. Well, I'm gonna turn in. Maybe something'll happen tomorrow. I hope not but in a way I hope so. G'night."

Eastern sky was just starting to lighten, enough to see silhouettes. Ben heard hooves and opened his eyes but didn't stir. He moved his head cautiously and saw a riderless horse. Standing not three feet from him. Saddled and ready to go, reins drooping on the ground. The steed looked at him imploring and expectant.

He got up slowly, kicked Cow lightly. "We have company!"

Cow started, sat up slowly, taking it in.

"That guy is wearing a nice saddle."

Ben approached the horse, cooing softly. "Here now, boy, what are you doing out here all alone? Where's your rider?"

He patted its neck, slowly leaning into the contact. The horse leaned in too. It seemed fit and unhurt, just relieved to find a person.

Cow put a few twigs on the fire to test if the bed was still hot; it was. Then coffee and water went into the coffee pot and he set it on the coals.

"Coffee coming in a few minutes."

His announcement was drowned out by another voice.

"There's that damn animal! Hands off my horse!"

A horse with two riders barreled in and stopped. A woman in front, and a man cursing the horse behind her. He jumped off and grabbed the reins.

Cow had a hand on his .45, staring at the newcomers. He pulled it out but didn't raise it.

Ben smiled icily. "Your horse, huh? You must be some horseman to let him wander into our camp. Fully saddled and all alone."

The woman dismounted slowly. "I can't disagree with that, Pete." She pointedly held her empty hands out, glancing at Cow's revolver. Her smile was sickly and concerned. "What are you two doing out here?"

"Minding our own business. Or at least we were until we were interrupted by a nice horse and two not so nice riders."

"Point taken. Can we have some of that coffee? Sit down and talk?"

Ben and Cow exchanged a glance. Cow nodded and holstered his pistol but he did keep a hand on it. The man stepped away from the horse, making the effort to show his hands.

Ben chuckled. "We only have two mugs. You can have a bowl. Or if you have mugs packed away, dig 'em out."

The man looked glad to have a task. He fumbled two coffee cups from his horse's saddle bags.

They sipped their joe, each wondering what the others were about. Ben decided to open.

"We work for Jerome Cobbson. Wants us to scout for intruders on his range. You?"

"Cobbson! Really!?"

"By the way, I'm Frank and that's Orv." He had no intention of giving real names, not yet.

"I'm Izzy, he's Pete. And we're doing the same thing."

"Oh?"

Ben let the question lie. Curiouser and curiouser. Why on earth was the old guy sending people out on duplicate jobs?

Cow spat out a few coffee grounds. That got the intruders to looking at him.

"Could be he wants us to find something, some stock or rustlers. Like he told us to do. Say, what's he paying you?"

Izzy looked at Pete. "Good money. Much more than we can make most anywhere around here. Why?"

"Us too. Don't make sense." Conversation lagged as they all chewed on that fact.

Clearing his throat, Cow went on. "You know, maybe it is all a smoke screen. Just wants to say he had… people out looking, if something should happen." Cow almost said 'men out looking' but caught himself.

"That may be." Izzy looked at her partner. "That could explain why he was in such a hurry to get us out here. Paid us some money up front and practically ushered us out of town. Told us where to go look."

Ben nodded. "Us too. Made a point of sending us north and west. The question is, did he want to be sure we would or wouldn't find cattle and funny business? We sure as heck haven't seen anything. Nothing but sagebrush and evergreens. Oh, and a coyote yesterday."

He looked at the guests and smiled then deadpanned. "Except for seeing a fine horse wandering the woods!"

Cow laughed at that. After a moment, so did Izzy, then Pete.

Cow laughed harder. "You know what? We should go back, separately. Raise our own smokescreen. Tell him we saw cattle here and there. And several different groups of cowpokes working them. But we just couldn't get close enough to see who or what was going on. All over this area!"

Ben smiled. "Give him something to scratch his head over. Collect our money and get out of town."

Pete scowled. "Not us. We'll look some more then go back and give an honest report—cattle and cowpokes scarce no matter how hard we rode." Izzy kind of nodded in agreement.

"Suit yourselves. I am beginning to think we're running a fool's errand. Why, isn't clear." Ben tossed his cold coffee with grounds onto the fire. The hiss and smoke was hypnotic for a few moments.

The intruders stood, repacked their coffee cups.

"Right. Well, we'll be going. Thanks for the coffee and the chat. And seeing to our horse. Good luck, safe riding." Izzy swung onto her horse. Pete got on, not as gracefully. They waved and cantered away, to the north and west.

Cow watched them disappear. "I don't know what to believe."

"Me neither. Us, we need to beat them back to town. Let's saddle up."

They were about ready to head out when the other two returned. They pulled up and dismounted. Pete reached with one hand inside his shirt. Incredibly, Izzy did the same.

Each held a something they couldn't discern; Ben wondered how fast he or Cow could reach the .45. They were firmly holstered. Cow had his buckled on and Ben's was hanging on a saddle horn.

Pete calmly talked and made no sudden moves.

"We were hired by Jerome Cobbson, yeah, to 'go find calves and rustlers'."

He stopped, looking at each man in turn. "But we are, that is I am, really a livestock inspector. We're State officers. She's a womens' deputy on temporary loan to the livestock branch. All under cover. So keep your traps shut. We're taking a risk telling you this." He glared when saying this last part. At that, he and the woman each flashed not a pistol but a badge.

Izzy took over. "We thought you guys were plants to track us. But your idea to go report false information convinced us you two are just pawns in Cobbson's game."

Ben sauntered over and buckled on his sidearm. This was getting weird and he wanted to do something to feel safe.

"You two. First you send in a horse. Then drop in out of nowhere. Leave and return. You tell good stories. What is the truth? Hell, this is becoming a hall of mirrors."

Cow stood near his horse, hand on the shotgun. Ben glanced over at Pete. Izzy sat on her horse, alert, tense, a hand lightly on a holstered pistol.

"How about I get a look at that badge? If you are who you say, what the heck is this 'game'? Is rustling such a problem, to call for work under cover? Who ever thought that up?"

Pete held out the badge, offered it to Ben. He held it up to light, turned it over. There he saw and memorized a serial number. That likely made it, and Pete, genuine.

Ben was relieved, and raised his hands to show openness. "Thanks. Alright now. There's more to our story too."

Cow jumped in. "We're miners just sent away from Cripple Creek. The Union started a war up there and we got shipped out with no warning. We are trying to get back home but need money. Cobbson had us doing farm work. Then made us a good offer to go out and ride around for a week."

Ben took over. "So we took him up on it. Neither of us set out to make things right on the range. We just need some cash. Truth be told, we didn't then and don't now like this. We surely hope we do not encounter any livestock or cowboys or rustlers."

Izzy swung off her horse and stood, one hand petting her horse's neck. "Well, they are out there alright. Rustlers. And cattle theft is big business. Just ask Pete. Figure each rancher loses two or three cattle a year at eighteen or twenty dollars per head. Take that times most all the ranches, hundreds and hundreds of 'em. It adds up to many of thousands of dollars going out the door."

Cow grinned, not amused. "Jeez Izzy. This is, like Ben said, a hall of mirrors."

She noted the name change but said nothing. Cow was still talking. "What should we do? Go, collect our wages, leave? Ride out again for Cobbson with no intention of finding anything? Try to help you guys?"

Ben jumped in. "Just had a nasty thought. Cobbson could be setting me and Cow up—couple of guys no one knows, have cash and guns. All of a sudden he could drop some stolen or questionable cattle on us. And then a posse. And we'd be swinging from a tree in no time."

Cow scuffed his feet. "Nah. Why do that?" He thought a minute. "I guess there are reasons to do that. To draw attention away from his other efforts, under the table agreements or something? Maybe he is in cahoots with some rustlers, or something. Or maybe he wants to gain traction with the sheriff?"

Izzy grinned. "Traction? What the heck is that? What do you mean, Cow or Orv or whatever you call yourself?"

"Credibility. Maybe he's trying to build credibility, trying to get in good with the sheriff. Who knows, but this whole thing smells. The more we talk on it the more I want to cut and run."

Cow looked at Ben, ignoring the law folks.

"I think we ought to get our pay—if we can do it easily—and get the heck out of the county. Forget the pay if we have to, but get out of here."

The womens' police officer smiled icily. "You go and do what you think needs done. Us, we're out here to find the bad guys. But far as we're concerned, we never saw you. And you never saw us, right?"

Ben and Cow nodded. Ben: "Hey, we've seen nothing but sagebrush and coyotes the last few days. Ain't seen no one. But if we had, we'd have wished them good luck."

V

Back at the Cobbson place, they gave their negative report: "Lots of riding, saw nothing but sagebrush. No cattle, calves, or people.

The boss man took it in stride. "Well, you go back out to that same general area. Look around and look hard. Someone is busy out there stealing my cattle. And I want it stopped."

The two exchanged glances. "Yes sir, we'll do that. We'll go scour the country to the north. One thing, can you give us a letter naming us?"

"Naming you? What do you mean? What for?"

Ben smiled warily. "We don't want to get taken for being out for ourselves or something like that. We want something to show the Sheriff or a posse if one does somehow meet up with us. You can't be too careful..."

A day or so later, the two again rode north. Cobbson did give them a letter. And fresh horses and left the firearms with them. They felt well prepared. Ambling side by side they talked.

"That was a darn good deal you worked, Ben. Getting him to say, in writing, who we are and what we're doing."

"Well, I figured, what's that old saying, 'better to be inside the tent pissing out than outside pissing in'."

"You just made that up!" Cow had to chuckle at the trail humor.

"Nah, it was a favorite saying of my dad's. I never understood it as a kid but sure do now. Anyway, this way we can ride where we want. Every so often we'll let him know we haven't found any strays. But you and me, we know, we ain't after calves or mama cows. Oh, we'll make a show of riding around. Will check into a canyon and up a mountain or two. Lots of those out here."

Cow smiled. "Riding around learning the country. Not a bad way to get paid."

Ben shrugged. "But we're really going out to look at mining towns. For the right job."

"Sooner or later he'll fire us." Cow frowned. "And I worry about Pete and Izzy. Out there riding around. Course, I guess that is what we're doing. Come to think of it, they have a badge to rely on. Can pull it out if they get in a jam. We can't do that."

"Let him. Fire us that is. We're up here in southern Colorado. Heading north. Riding good horses we can prove we have by right. Armed. With a week's worth of grub. And a bottle of Raton Lightning!"

"Yeah, I think we're in pretty good shape."

Ben went on, ignoring the interruption.

"If he wants to get rid of us, what's he gonna do, send a posse after us? For being incompetent livestock detectives? Worst that happens is we have to pay something for the horses. Doubt he'll go to the trouble, especially since we will be good sincere employees who report in regularly."

He spurred the horse and it ran ahead a few steps then slowed. He waved his hat. "Yeehaw! I just wish some pink would give me the evil eye right now. I'd love to make one of those snakes look down the double barrels for a change..."

Cow caught up.

"Hey Ben. Relax. Don't get cocky just 'cause you got a horse and a shotgun. We do not want a fight with the pinks, or anyone else. This is serious business. Let's just play it cool while we check out mines. We have money and supplies and a good story. Let's not mess it up."

Cow stopped. "Seriously, Ben. There are lots of mine camps up this way that we can stop in for a look see."

His companion nodded. "Yeah, there's Creede, maybe Lake City, Gunnison and Crested Butte, Bonanza, even the Orient Mine east of Villa Grove."

Just then two riders came over the hill from the north, moving steady but not fast. They pulled up, apparently ready to chat. An older man gave a friendly smile and burst forth with gossip, questions and news.

"Hello! How's the way south? Where you come from?"

Before either could reply, he went on. Clearly he was starved for company. "Say, did you hear about the train wreck over near Pueblo? A train bound for the World's Fair in Saint Louis was crossing a river just outside of town. Fountain Creek I hear it was called. The trestle gave way and most of the train went in. Seventy some people killed. Awful. So where'd you say you were from? How's the road south? Oh say, my friend here don't talk. He is deaf and dumb. Good with the horse though..."

The man was clearly ready for conversation. Ben was vaguely aware of the World's Fair. It made sense special trains would take folks there.

"No, we hadn't heard about the train. Sad news indeed."

Cow jumped in before he man could get started again. "We're heading north from the Raton-Taos area. Trail is pretty clear and easy. Where you coming from? Say, have you seen any stray calves? Or mamas looking for their calves?"

Cow may as well have smacked the man with a trout. His eyes narrowed and the smile vanished.

"Raton, huh? Asking about cattle? We ain't stupid, you know. Are you tied up with that Cobbson crook? He has crews out everywhere looking for 'stray' calves to rustle. Likely story!"

"Good day," he said with a venomous voice.

He turned to his companion and gestured with his hands, communicating somehow. The deaf man suddenly looked hostile and he put a hand on his holstered pistol before grabbing his reins. The two of them rode away, fast, with not another word.

"Well. That was... interesting. If we meet people I guess we had better ask about mine camps not calves."

Ben nodded, watching to be sure the two riders in fact did go on over the hill. He listened for a moment for the hoof beats to continue heading south.

"Yeah. Old farmer Cobbson cuts a wide swath. Rustling must be big business."

"It might make sense to swap these horses. They have his brand. We need to blend in better, judging from that little set to."

"Good idea, Cow. Let's head for Creede. Maybe there'll be a stable in Del Norte willing to give us two fresh nags for these." He paused. "Or we can play the game. Just alter the brand a little to make it ours."

"Doing that would make it easier to swap. Or maybe then we wouldn't have to." Cow looked excitedly at Ben.

"My point exactly. Not sure about doing it but that is an option."

They hadn't ridden more than twenty yards. Ben pulled up. "No. That is a bad idea. Sure, it was me who suggested changing the brand. That is just plain stupid. Not a good road to head down. If we get started with that we could soon find ourselves hanging by the neck until dead. The law would catch us. Or Cobbson and his rustlers would. They wouldn't take lightly to us crowding into their game. Those guys all play for keeps."

He looked at Cow and went on. " We don't want in on that game. Let's just go on checking mine camps and being dumb and innocent if someone brings up cattle, calves, or Cobbson."

Cow smiled wickedly. "C'mon Ben, it'd be easy. Just heat an iron or even a knife and press in one or two marks."

"Real easy at first but difficult and crazy as hell later. Count me out."

He gazed at Cow, unblinking, until Cow looked away.

He felt better making the decision, and was ready to move out.

"Let's go to Antonito. That town in the southern San Luis Valley is a crossroads. From there we can catch a train to Alamosa and Creede." Kneeing his horse gently, it started off.

Cow watched, shook his head, and followed.

A DAY LATER.

"Alright, here's Antonito. We can take a train now! Where do you want to go? I'm thinking Creede then maybe

Silverton or Saguache. From there we can check Bonanza gold camp and the iron mine."

"Iron? This old Cowman is a gold and silver man. What is this about iron?"

"Yeah, there is an iron ore mine. Limonite, I guess, whatever variety of iron they get from that ore. It is near Villa Grove in the north end of the Valley. Bonanza is a few miles northwest of Villa Grove, the Orient mine is northeast."

Cow shrugged. "I just don't know. Not sure I want to go back to the mine."

"Well hell. We can't ride around forever pretending to be cowboys. I want to get back with my girl in Cripple or somewhere. And back to real life. What besides mining work are you going to do, Cow? Your family needs food and clothes. Can you run a store or work wood or metal or a tannery or run a farm? What can we do? Like Mrs. Cobbson said, we each of us need to decide what to do with ourselves. Cobbson's choice, you could say!"

Cow groaned. "Yeah, I guess. But I'm not sure."

"Me neither. But I have to go look. Could be we can get on at a mine. Or even in on a mine, who knows. Somewhere we can find an opportunity, some other way to make money. What Abby sent me is starting to run a little low. I have to get something going."

Cow hesitated. "Well, we can take a train from here to Villa Grove and the mines up north. Or west to Creede. Maybe east to Walsenburg and the coal mines around Trinidad."

Ben shrugged. "Yeah. Check out mine jobs, if Hamlin doesn't interfere. Then we need to get with family, those who stayed in Cripple when we got shipped out."

"Yup. We're not on Mister Hamlin's list, but we sure are on his blacklist."

They both thought about Mr. Clarence Hamlin. He was secretary of the Cripple Creek Mine Owners Association, the CCMOA. He kept a list there of men who agreed not to join the WFM, the Western Federation of Miners. That was general, public knowledge. There was an open secret around this. The MOA also kept a 'blacklist', a tally of known WFA members and sympathizers. Those men were marked and could not get job at most mines. And the CCMOA made sure to keep regional mine owners informed of both registers. Hamlin and his lists lurked in mens' minds, much as would the Selective Service Draft live in their grandsons' minds. It was a shadow they had to keep in mind and know where they stood with it at all times.

"Let's flip a coin to decide where to go."

AT ABOUT THAT TIME AND SEVERAL MOUNTAIN RANGES AWAY, two other people, siblings, were also making decisions.

Brother and sister, they weren't on the run out of northern New Mexico. Rather they were home in Cripple Creek, about thirty miles southwest of Colorado Springs. The camp sat in a high volcanic valley. Pikes Peak glowered to the northeast, sometimes sunny and sometimes cloud obscured. That often presaged a show with lightning caroming off the rocks and thunder growling.

Abby Bosini was home from her teaching. Trying to relax. She couldn't, for worry over her friend and lover Ben McNall. Who apparently was stranded in New Mexico. And apparently consorting with some man Frank Mack. She wondered how he and Ben met, and what hold Mack had on Ben. Whatever the problem, and there were plenty of them, she worried. A few days ago she sent as many dollars as she could scrape up. No word since.

The school year was almost over; students would be out in just a few days. Her contract for the next year was ready to be signed. She mused and worried on the students who had left recently. Classes were noticeably quieter and smaller now.

Cripple Creek had changed since the explosion. The owners' reaction to that had been to round up all the union sympathizers they could find and ship them away.

Many people were forced out in tumult with the camp tearing at itself. Others had left of their own accord. Somehow the place was now less dynamic and not so adventurous.

Ben along with many other union men was forcibly escorted out. For that matter, many sympathizers, not members but just people known to favor the miners' union, got it too. They were all deported out to, just past, the state line. 'Deported'. As if they were traitors or common hobos or criminals. Maybe they were in Kansas, maybe New Mexico. Hell, maybe Wyoming. Who knew? Good information hard to come by.

After the deportations and tumult things quieted down. The miners' union with all the violence and turbulence it generated had been defanged. It was not so much a feared and violent part of camp living.

Life was less dangerous now, with explosions, beatings and confrontations a thing of the past. Even so, many miners and merchants were leaving. Population was shrinking, jobs were disappearing, houses and businesses stood vacant. The 'greatest gold camp on earth' was still a formidable wealth creator. But rather than growing and improving, it was stagnating, maybe even edging backwards.

THE YOUNG WOMAN WATCHED HER BROTHER LON OPEN THE front door. She still sometimes marveled that he was a tall guy with dirty blond hair and blue eyes. They wouldn't be taken as siblings. She too was tall but her dark hair and brown eyes belied their kinship. Their father was Italian, their mother Irish. That alone made for interesting family dynamics, loving but volatile, practical but somehow dramatic. Lon and Abby each had some of their parent's traits.

Several years ago Abby had come to Cripple Creek to teach. She was comfortable in the classroom and community. To students she was able and popular but no pushover. To parents she was a source of knowledge and a bulwark of firm compassion.

Her older brother Lon followed her to the gold camp. He had an entrepreneur's eye for geology. It took him just a few months to prospect, claim, and develop the Double I Mine. It was a good vein they tapped. The income paid the Bosinis' expenses with money left over. In Cripple it was a modest property; in many mining towns it would have been king of the roost.

Lon smiled and handed her a 'gram from Farmers State Bank in Raton NM. It said simply,

MONEY WIRE REC'D AND PAID.

"He has the money, Ab. So now what?"

"So now I find out where he is. Ben. Also see who this Frank Mack is and how he fits in. And I want to join him. Ben, that is. Not the Mack character."

"Give up your teacher job? Really?" He sat and looked his sister in the eye, gazing for probably half a minute. His mind raced. "Abby, I do not want to leave Cripple. I love running the mine and I love the town, warts and all."

"I'm not surprised. You need to stay, Lon. I'll tell them I'm not renewing this week, and…"

"Before you go off and do that, Abby, think it through. Stall on signing. I don't think you want to burn that bridge yet. Maybe you need to find out where he is and when—if—he can meet you. And what he intends to do now. Remember, he could have stayed but he just couldn't step away from that damned union."

"I don't care, Lon. I can teach anywhere, and I am going to find Ben."

VI

IN ANTONITO, THE WANDERING EX MINERS PONDERED AND stalled. Finally a coin toss sent them west. They figured to try Creede. From there they could go on to Silverton or Lake City, or return east to Antonito.

AS THE TRAIN APPROACHED TOWN, BEN QUOTED A REMEM-bered verse. "Its day all day in the daytime and there is no night in Creede!"

"Is that so, Ben? No night? Looks to me like this train we're on is riding into the sunset."

"Cow, I thought you attended a fancy day school back east. Didn't you study literature?"

Cow thought, grinned. "Let's just say that I heard it discussed."

Ben grinned too. "That line is from a well known poem. This Creede place was a real goin' jenny in the 80s and early 90s. You know, when silver was booming. Like many camps, things never closed down. The mines ran twenty four hours. And, as the man said, so did the pool halls, bars and bordellos."

"Well, it looks to me like Jenny was goin', alright. She headed out of town. Went somewhere else. And she took most of the lights with her." Cow looked around, shrugged. "There sure is night in Creede now!"

"Yah. Probably darn few jobs here, mining or mine related. Maybe a job as a pink." Ben's expression was bleak.

He grabbed a seat as the engine slowed then lurched to a stop. He looked around and continued his thought.

"Come to think of it, I bet there is darn little work. Of any kind." Ben laughed mirthlessly. "You got it right about Jenny. If she is still here, if Jenny hasn't left town, somebody better call a priest. 'Cause she needs her Last Rites."

A conductor bounced down the aisle, grabbing each seat by the corner as he announced the location.

"Creede, Colorado. Train will depart in twenty three minutes, twenty three." Doors opened, whistles blew, and the few passengers got off.

Ben reached for his new small knapsack. He hoped most of his stuff was still safe in Cripple but doubted it. All he owned for sure was in that canvas bag with shoulder straps: a change of clothes, pen and notebook, and a jacket. All that, and the bag, he had bought in Raton with some of the money Abby had wired. What little remained of that windfall was strapped to his chest under his shirt.

"We spent more than I wanted to come up here. Let's get off and see what..."

SOMEONE CLIMBED INTO THE RAIL CAR. BEN WAS SILENCED BY the vision. He—it?—was tall and skinny, with long arms and legs. And a huge moustache—it drooped past his chin. The person had to be well over six and a half feet tall. And looked to tip the scales at maybe one forty. He thought that Mrs. Cobbson back in Raton weighed in at more than that, and he grinned in spite of himself.

The big Stetson hat made him look like a clad skeleton from Mexico's Day of the Dead. Tall, gangly, a big hat, a face with farcical moustache on skin drawn tight over the skull. There was some little flesh on the bones. He carried two big pearl handled Colt .45's in holsters. These were big, the barrels looking to be fifteen inches or so. Ben wondered how such a skinny thing had the strength to tote those two hog legs. Much less pull and fire one of them!

Tiny eyes peered from under the Stetson, and a voice shrilled, "Boy, why are ya grinnin' at the Shaff...?"

The New England twang took them by surprise. In a dying southwest Colorado mining town, a Bostonian nasal whine?

Cow laughed, unable to stop himself. After a moment it came clear that he was the Sheriff, the local lawman.

The Shaff put a hand on one of the .45s, the left side.

"What's so dang funny, you? One grins, the other laughs? Ya are getting off on the wrong foot with me."

He squinted. "Ah tell ya, Ah'm the Shaff here in Creede. Nothin' happens unless Ah say it can. And Ah meet every train. You two ain't miners, ah ya? Ya look like hahd rock men."

He pulled the .45 out, holding it loosely, dangling, not aiming it.

"An mah job is to turn miners raht around. We don't want no more miners heah."

Cow smothered another giggle. He sat back on the seat and fixed the man with a smile. Showed his hands in submission.

"Well, Shaff, I mean Sheriff, we're not laughing at ya. The thing is, your accent reminds me of my grandmother. She lived, God rest her soul, on Beacon Hill there in Boston. I visited her and my grandpa every summer. Hearing a New Englander's talk brought back many memories."

He cleared his throat. 'Mostly good ones as you probably imagine."

He paused, smiled, nodded at the lawman, then went on.

"And, yeah, we both have mining experience. Come to see what is going on here in Creede. And maybe we are wanting to look for work. Of some kind. I guess there aren't many mining jobs up here, no? How about other jobs?"

The skeletal form holstered the pistol. Again, Ben wondered how he had the strength to manhandle such a piece.

The Shaff looked surprised, nonplused, at the unexpected New England connection. He was not quite sure what to do. The double negative threw him off. The lawman was a good rule follower. The city fathers knew this which is why he had blanket instructions to run off any miners coming in. But he wasn't good at picking up on mangled grammar.

Ben wasn't sure if it was a smile or a grimace that the man fixed on his face. In fact the lawman was intrigued that someone had a Boston connection.

"Heyll no. Ain't no jobs in Creede, 'less you want to pick through tailings piles or chase stray dogs off of claims or some such. Maybe a rancher down the valley will let you sleep in the barn if you pitch hay for a day."

He turned and started to walk. Stopped.

"Matter of fact, Ah did hear of something. You boys know anything about cattle?"

Ben and Cow exchanged an apprehensive glance.

Cow shrugged. "Well…"

"Ah mean cattle brands and branding, not those stupid four legged critters."

Ben didn't want to tick this guy off. No telling how those big .45s might get used. He swallowed his surprise and answered mildly.

"Ranchers mark their stock with a sign, seared on the calves when they're babes. I don't know…"

Cow broke in. "Well, Shaff—can I call you that or do you have a name? Anyway, yes, my friend is right. The state keeps, or is supposed to keep, a log of each rancher's brand."

Ben went on. "We heard a lot about this down Raton way. Some man named Cobbson was looking for branded and unbranded cattle. Have you heard of him?"

"'W' heyll, you two may be miners but you ain't complete stupid. Yeah, I've heard of Cobbson. Who hasn't? He's big in the cattle trade—working both over and under the table, some say. He talked to you two?"

He ignored his question and looked at Cow. "My name back in Boston is Henry Cabot Roush."

Cow nodded. "So you're one of THE Cabots?" He glanced at Ben. "Prominent Mayflower family, don't you know?"

The gangly man nodded. "Ayuh. My mother is—was—a Cabot. That stuffy group made me want to leave town. Which I did a few yeahs back. And came out and now I'm the Shaff. That's what I go by, Shaff. Now, let me tell you…"

He looked around to see if anyone was watching.

"Ah'm supposed to send you packing. March you right back on the train and get you out of town."

Ben called him on it. "But you don't want to. Isn't that right, Shaff?"

"Right. Heyll, ya are just men looking for work. Can't fault that. What are you willing to do? Ore sorting? Wash dishes and mop floors at the café?"

He smirked. "Ah know. Security guard at a mine!" He shrieked a laugh. Ben was reminded of a raccoon he had found in a trap, foot bloody and clamped, howling in pain and terror.

"Nah, really. You want to avoid that don't ya?" Another shriek. "Ya got to watch them guys. Pinkertons and the like, thugs hired by mine owners and other rich bastahds. Them men are on the lookout for ya returning miners, men that got deported or fired. They'd as soon shoot as look at ya. But I bet ya know that..." He chuckled, this time low and intense not a trapped animal cry.

Again he glanced around.

"Are ya willing to do whatever needs done? I may have an idea. Working cattle brands. Tell me..."

A short squat man with an engineer's cap strode into the station.

"Sheriff, how are you?" He looked at the recent arrivals. "And who are these men?" He turned to face the two. "Are you miners?"

Ben shrugged. "No, not any more we're not."

"Not any more, huh? You are miners!"

The man took his cap off and twisted it into a ball. He looked at the Sheriff and back at Ben.

"I am the Mayor. As the Sheriff no doubt said, you are not welcome in Creede."

He spoke briskly to the Sheriff. Surprisingly he fell into the man's slang.

"Put them back on the train, Shaff. See that they leave town, then come see me. We need to talk." He strode away, assuming instant obedience.

Sheriff Cabot Roush shrugged. "Well, that does it. Ya gotta go, ya gotta. Can't stay. But think about this: If you know cattle brands, ya probably know about shading them. Do ya?"

"Shading?"

"Oh come on! Don't play innocent. Change the brand—the brand with a V becomes an X and bam! You have yourself a calf. Something to build a herd on." Another shriek rang out and he winked. "That works wonders if you are careful to start with. Just an idea for you ex-miners!"

"I don't know...

He walked towards the train, urging them towards the door. Looking around one last time, with voice low like the chuckle. "It is a good way to build a life. I can't live on my salary. But trust me, I know shading can work. Ya didn't hear that here and I'll shoot ya myself if you try to say so."

Straightening up, he returned to being the Shaff and spoke loudly. "Well jennamen. Time to go. We wish you the best of luck with your search. Just search somewhere else. As the Mayor said, there isn't room here in Creede for two more miners. Even if one is from Boston! I need ya to get on that train."

In full sheriff mode, his hand again rested on one of his .45s. He meant business—his eyes squinched even smaller. They moved toward the car.

Even years later, this scene would from time to time appear, unbidden, in Ben's mind. Every fall when he saw or read of the Mexicans' celebration of Dia de Los Muertos, he thought of that skeletal man, serious, hand brushing a holster, and that moment.

But those memories would appear in the future, not the gritty present. Now, Ben and Cow meekly obeyed. They climbed into the car as the whistle blew. Down the valley the engine started, train clanking and creaking.

Before the door closed, the Bostonian spoke again, this time kindly. "Ya remember what ah said about building a life. Give it some thought. It is a tough time to be a miner and there are other things to do. Good luck!"

Shaff Cabot lifted his hat in salute. Ben was surprised he didn't use both hands, as big as it was.

The tall figure then turned and headed away, praying mantis like. Ben wondered if he went in search of or to avoid the Mayor.

Cow smiled slowly. "Shading. Weird, that is the last thing I'd expect a lawman to suggest. I wonder if we ought to try it."

"Come on, Cow. Get real. We already covered this. Sure, if you're lucky maybe you can pick up a calf or two. But any rancher or hired hand who catches you will make short work. He won't call the Sheriff, he'll shoot or hang you. It just ain't worth it, my friend.

Cow nodded thoughtfully. "You're probably right, Ben."

Relieved, Ben went on. "That whole experience was odd. As expected, there's no future here for us."

"Didn't take long to find that out, did it?"

Ben went on. "Your Mayflower man was a real character."

"Yeah, you have to wonder—he seemed to slip a cog or two. Maybe too many cousins married in his lineage...?"

Ben guffawed. "I bet ol' Shaff Cabot or whoever he really is didn't run to escape Boston's stuffiness. More likely he got out of town just ahead of a judge's gavel!"

"Or a furious father waving a shotgun."

The rhythm of the tracks took over. They watched the country slip by.

VII

Ben loved the glow of Colorado autumns. He couldn't believe he—and Abby and their new kids—had been in Nederland, a little mountain town, for almost a decade.

Yes, he thought, up here the season was wonderful but short lived. Their fine little mountain town was sliding into winter. The calendar showed late September. You could find morning ice along the creek these days. The aspen leaves had turned golden. They glowed and flaunted their attire to any and all during fine sunny blue sky days. Before long the winds would knock leaves to the ground. Shriveled and brown, they would make piles and drifts just like the snow which would come to bury them.

Those winds, Ben knew, would soon bring blizzards. Arctic air would howl and slice through town. Looking out the kitchen window, he imagined—and remembered—snow up to the panes.

He looked away, smiled as Abby entered, herding and seating their twins.

"Morning Buster. Morning Ace. How'd you sleep?"

"Ben. I thought we agreed to use names not nicknames."

"You're right, Ab. Sorry." He turned to the children. "Good morning, Rutherford. Good morning, Marie. Did you sleep well?"

Both nodded sleepily, poking at their oatmeal bowls.

Ben smiled at Rutherford Hayes McNall and Marie Curie Mcnall. For now, they ignored him, concentrating on breakfast.

While pregnant, Abby had insisted they carry on his family's tradition of naming children for famous people. Ben liked the idea. But now that he had kids, he had to admit that he preferred calling them Buster and Ace. He felt the nicknames captured the kid's personalities better than the lengthy given ones.

"Well Abby, fall is here, ready or not." He glanced at the newspaper. "I see the autumn traditions of celebrating in Mexico go on. Dia de Los Muertos is coming up." For a moment he was quiet, reliving the old scene with that sheriff from Creede: He always saw the dingy mining town in the background and the man's skeletal stance with huge Stetson. The taut expression, friendly then aggressive and the strange gestures remained clear.

"Thinking about Creede again?" Abby smiled.

"Yup. Odd unique and sticky memory, that one." He shook his head and banished it back to memory. Mine maintenance items came to mind.

"The big winter winds will come soon. Usually about this time. I need to be sure the power lines are up to the conditions. Rutherford! Stop that!"

Abby glanced over then grabbed a spoon and put it down wordlessly by the boy's bowl.

"Yes Ben, I agree, we need to make sure of that. How will you do it?"

"A friend of a friend told me about a guy. Someone knows him and he's a lineman for Boulder Power and Light. Name of Ted Moore, a longtime resident of the area. I guess he did a ride by of that guy's power poles and so forth. And he gave some pointers to make things go better. I'll get in touch and maybe we can get him to do that for us. I'd be willing to pay a fee, or at least buy him lunch or dinner."

"Sounds good," she nodded. "Marie! Finish your breakfast. We're going to visit your Uncle Lon today. I need for you and your brother to finish up and go get dressed. We're going to take the train."

MENTION OF LON MADE BEN MUSE. HERE HE AND ABBY WERE, married with kids, well into the new century. And they were successful miners in the Nederland gold fields! Thirty miles west of Boulder, fifty northwest of Denver. Mine owners, who would have thought that a few years back?

Things were going well at their Deportati Mine. After some talk, they had settled on that name, Italian for 'deported'. The choice was meant to thumb a nose at the Cripple Creek Mine Owners' Association. They had done it. The men who had entrained and sent him away in disgrace now had a competitor. Maybe the Ned mines weren't the 'greatest gold camp on earth' but it was treating them well, thank you very much. The Deportati was perhaps not a heavyweight player on the national scene. But it was a steady competitor nonetheless.

The Deportati's start and success was thanks to Lon' and Abby's financial backing. And Ben's hard work.

Ben for one never ever thought he'd be an owner. Couldn't have imagined he'd be looking over the desk at the daily workers who actually handled the rock and ore and dynamite. Even today he considered himself a miner first, owner later.

This train of thought ran cattywampus. Other memories crowded into the kitchen, and the twins' ruckus receded.

HIS MIND'S EYE—AND EAR—WERE FLOODED. HE DRIFTED back through years:

He and Cow on the train from Creede to the San Luis Valley. Looking at other mining camps. The gist of other experiences, sights, and people came flowing back. And always the two miners were looking over their shoulders for, and occasionally seeing, pinks. Intermittent ranch or farm work, with no pinks. Some of those farm men were rough, ready to look for trouble. At least the pinks pretty much left you alone if you stayed out of the mining camps.

Finally he remembered washing up in Denver with Abby. And at some point Cow decided to stay on a ranch. He still wasn't sure about all of his friend's journey.

ABBY SAT AND WATCHED HIM SWIM IN THE POOL OF DEEP thought and memory. She poured herself a cup of coffee.

Ben heard her ask if he wanted a warm up, which brought him back to Nederland.

"Uh, no, no thanks. I need to get going. I'll try to run down the power line man. I need to get on that. And I'm going—or sending George—to the assay office."

Intrigued and excited, she asked, "What are we assaying, Ben? I don't remember a new branch of the vein? Or what, something else? I thought we had a good vein of ore."

"Oh, we do, for gold."

"But?"

"Abby, I'm after that black sludge we have so much of. We finally had someone look at that. You and I talked on having that done. Your keeping up with the mad duo here," he smiled at their twins as he continued "it may have slipped your mind. Please keep that under your bonnet. By all means tell Lon and ask him not to say anything too."

"Of course. I need to get going myself. You have a good day."

FOR SOME REASON HE COULDN'T SHAKE OLD MEMORIES THIS day. He wondered what his old friend Cow was up to.

On the way to the assay office he stopped in for another cup of coffee at the café.

He saw his friend, George Mason, a native of the area. "Those winter winds will be here soon."

"Yup."

"You know, Ben, I have a theory about why this valley is so windy."

"Oh?"

"The continental divide is just a few miles west of town, right? Well, Rollins Pass, the railroad pass just west of here, goes over the furthest east point. Nowhere in North America is the divide any further east. And the ridges are very low there. Not even 12000'. So we are sitting down wind from a huge natural funnel. For snow and especially wind, concentrating the natural west to east air flow. Thus the winter gusts."

"Makes sense." Ben nodded.

"Have you been reading the paper, Ben? Let me guess what they are saying: Race riots and lynchings in the south. Pogroms against Jews in Russia. Britain and Germany in a naval arms race. Teddy Roosevelt's Panama Canal coming along. Lots of immigrants coming in to America. Aeroplanes flying all over the country, stopping at towns. Automobile roads starting to be built everywhere. Volcanoes erupting, famine in China."

"That's about it, George. The world is always going to hell, no?" They laughed. "I did see an article on ranching. When it comes to nasty fighting, cattlemen and sheepmen put cats and dogs to shame. And mine investors get after each other some times. It says here..." Ben opened the paper. "I'll be damned. Cow Weston."

George looked and mostly acted like an old time miner, with fingers splayed from handling endless rock and receiving errant hammer blows, skin weathered, wiry and strong. Yet he daintily sipped his coffee as if sitting with the Queen. Normally amusing, right now Ben didn't even see it.

"Who? Cow? What kind of name is that?"

"Not his real name. it's a long story. Remember the mining labor wars in Cripple Creek back in '03 and '04? I was there. So was he, Cow."

"I did not know that, Mr. McNall."

Ben nodded, on a roll.

"The two of us, and many others, got deported from there after one of the explosions. Most of us, certainly Cow and I, had nothing to do with the violence. Didn't matter. We were known union sympathizers. We all, that is, pretty much all of us, got rounded up and sent away by train. Cow and I buddied up on the way. You needed someone watch your back. At least for a while. At first he and I worked some cattle and tried some mines but we drifted apart. Haven't heard of or seen Cow for years!"

"Deported, huh? I wondered about your mine name. The Deportati. That is Italian for deported, isn't it? Your and Abby's property. Ain't she part Italian?"

Ben nodded absently as he read the article, ignoring George, the other customers, and his short stack. He threw down the dog eared newspaper.

"Cow Weston. Wow. That name brings things back I tell you. So many memories, good and bad."

He sat, eyes vacantly looking at a coffee cup in his favorite Nederland cafe. The name transported him back to southern Colorado, years ago. A train ride in southwest Colorado.

He all but felt the rocking on the tracks, the engineer managing a nice coasting ride from Creede down to Del Norte. The conversation he had with Cow was clear as day.

"Well, no job in Creede. Just as well, old Shaff gave me the creeps."

Cow smiled. "Yeah, there's a story there we'll never know. He and the mayor can keep their sleepy dying town. Still, the guy with the sheriff's badge made to run us off. And then he goes out on a limb to hint about cattle rustling? Strange. That whole business intrigues me."

"Business? Hell, it isn't business, it is theft, pure and simple. Looks to me like a quick way to get strung up or beaten and run out of the state. Again. Yeah, it can be profitable I guess, but the potential cost is too high. For me." Ben paused and continued.

"Anyway, how about we go look at some of the camps up north. Bonanza has gold mines and isn't a huge camp like Cripple. Maybe we can get something going there. Let's take the train north, drop in on Saguache."

"Yeah, what is up with that place. Sa-goo-atchy, sa-goo-atch, whatever. Why you wanna go there?"

"Well, Cow, two reasons. First is I want to find something to do, make money, and it doesn't have to be mining. Maybe there's something there. A hotel or a freight service or a farm or something. Who knows?"

He shrugged. "And, I had a friend in Cripple. A good man named George Henderson. He was born and raised in Saguache. Said it was a nice little town. Sad to say, he died in the explosion that got us run out of town. I just want to look in on the place, maybe send a prayer his way."

"He sure didn't deserve that. No more that we deserved what we got."

"True that. And by the way, he told me 'saguache' is a word in the Ute language for 'blue earth'. There must be some strange patch of ground there. Or maybe it is a myth, who knows. That is just what he told me."

"Alright, Saguache then Bonanza it is. We can get our horses out of the stable in Del Norte. Ride them up that way. Or maybe I should say get the horses Cobbson provided."

"I'd say they are our horses now. Possession being nine tenths of the law and all. And we have that letter."

THE RIDE TO THE NORTH END OF THE SAN LUIS VALLEY seemed endless. The place was rolling flat, treeless, and it felt wide as the Atlantic. Except for the big mountains on both sides. They were glad to call in on Saguache, a nice interlude. Then they got on with the trek.

They rode east away from blue earth country. Cow rode easy with the sway as the horse ambled. "Well my friend, I have to say, Saguache wasn't much. Was it what you expected?"

"Not much to it," Ben agreed. "I guess before the railroad came, and bypassed it, the place was a thriving hub. You had to go through Saguache to get to Lake City mines or Gunnison ranches. But the iron horse withered it in short order. Still, I am glad and sad to have gone there and saluted my friend George's memory."

Cow nodded.

The little railroad town of Villa Grove soon hove into view. The road from Saguache came in from the south. From there they could go several directions. To get to Bonanza a road led off to the northwest. The road to the Orient mine led due east. The way north was to Salida and the Arkansas River. Villa Grove was a hub in and of itself, of roads and trails for ranchers and miners. The railroad made a stop there too.

A train looked to have just arrived from the south, from Alamosa. A group of men were getting horses off a livestock car. They acted disciplined and purposeful.

"That looks like a group on the hunt, Cow. I wonder what they're after."

One of the men looked their way, and promptly tapped another on the shoulder and pointed at them.

"They are looking over here. What do we do?"

Ben laughed. "Nothing. Just go about our business. You know, we're merely looking for strays for Cobbson. Can prove it. Let's go down to the turnoff and head up Bonanza way."

The group had saddled up and mounted. They came towards the deported miners.

"You two! Stop!"

Ben and Cow ignored this, riding towards the Bonanza road.

"I'm a deputy sheriff and I tell you to stop!" He fired a shot in the air.

The two stopped, intently but not overly quick as they rode up.

Ben turned. "I see you have a star. We are minding our own affairs. What is your business, sheriff?"

The group stopped, semi-surrounding the two, the leader looking them over. Neither made a move, just stared back.

"We are looking for some so called cattle men. One man flashes a badge and claims to be sheriff in Creede, another says he is the mayor.

"Ah hell, do you mean the Shaff? Big, tall weird looking guy, giant Stetson, carrying two hoglegs?" Cow exploded in laughter. "We saw him the other day. It was two or three days ago, maybe four. The two of them ran us out of their dingy Creede town. Don't tell me they were fakers!?"

"Fakers, no. Cattle rustlers, yes. Have you seen them? Any idea where they are?"

"Heck no. They made sure to get us on the train to Del Norte and that's the last we saw. What do you want 'em for? Rustling, you say?" Cow glanced at Ben.

"We haven't seen them, Sheriff. Or any men out and about. For that matter we have seen darn few cattle, fenced or unfenced. No strays."

Ben turned his horse. "If we see or hear anything of them we'll send word to the station master here at Villa Grove. Let's go, Orv."

He had no intention of giving real names to this group. Posse, hell, he thought. This smelled like a mob of vigilantes. They rode on, glad to put the 'posse' well behind them.

"Boy, this gold camp—Bonanza, right?—sure sits way up in a valley."

Cow peered up as they neared a settlement. "Yup, that mountain and its ridges sure look down on it. The map says that is Mount Antora."

"The whole valley looks dead to me, at least as far as mining and business go. Even if there is a pretty mountain up there."

Ben stopped by a building where a man sat, legs up on a chair, apparently enjoying a siesta. Or maybe he was drunk or nodding off. At a glance, hard to tell.

"Hey, you in the chair. Hello!"

The man opened his eyes, staring ahead for a moment. He took his legs down and creakily stood. "Aw hell, are you two more miners? Looking for work? You sure look like it. But you have nice horses. Most of you guys are on foot. You are miners, aren't ya?"

He stretched and sat back down. Spat. "You're wasting your time here. No mining jobs. Or other work, for that matter. Leastways, no honest work."

"Things are that bad, huh?" Cow glanced around, and saw only an empty street.

The man looked around. Not a soul to be seen.

"Yeah, it is that bad. Mines played out, mills closing, people moving on. Plus, lately there have been three of four Pinkertons hanging around town. If you are a deported miner they'd love to get their hands on you. After having some of their fun they'd run you out of the place."

He smiled. "Word to the wise and all—avoid men wearing neckties and fedoras. You probably know that! I was a miner but haven't touched hard rock for weeks. And I have never been deported—have avoided the black ball. Fat lot of good that does me! I still can't find work. Best of luck to you two."

He sat, put his legs back up. Pulling his hat down over his eyes, he dismissed Ben and Cow.

The two turned, unsure what next. The man lifted the hat and spoke. "I hear they are looking for men over at the Orient. Not hard rock mining, but a job is a job..." He smiled and drifted off.

THE HORSES AMBLED AND THEY TALKED. "ORIENT. THAT IS the mine east of Villa Grove, up on the west side of the Sangre De Cristos. What do you think? It is iron ore they're digging. Not hard rock underground. Maybe we can get on there. Then I can bring my family down." Cow looked over. "I'd like that."

Ben snorted. "Forget that pipe dream, my man. The Orient Mine is owned by the big steel mills in Pueblo. Colorado Fuel and Iron Company or some such name. The mine's ores go into the furnaces there. And guess what, do you know who owns those mills? The Rockefellers, that's who. If not them some of their rich friends."

Cow's smile faded. Ben was on to something.

"Hell, man, we're two schlubs on the run from Cripple. Do you think for a minute we have a chance of getting on there? Hell, their security will smell us a mile away. They don't need pinks. The Rockefellers and the other rich men have their own goons. They all but invented private security. And believe it, you and me won't even get near the place. We have a better chance of having the President name us Ambassadors to Paris."

Silent riding.

"Hell."

"Yeah."

"Let's catch the train at Villa. Go over the hill to Salida. Maybe we can meet up with our folks there." Ben's heart soared at seeing Abby.

Ben hated giving up but grudgingly said it anyway. "I guess mining is out. At least for a while. Maybe things'll settle down and we can get on somewhere."

Cow nodded, which Ben didn't see. "Yeah, things are darn sticky now for us. We're untouchable at least down in this part of the state. Damn Clarence Hamlin and his list."

He smiled at a thought. "Say, what about that shading. Brand shading or whatever he said. Old Sheff. Or Shaff, the skeleton with .45s. Odd thing for a lawman to bring up. Changing the brand on a calf or cow sounds... illegal. But it could be a quick way to make good money."

"Well, if we believe that posse or gang we saw, old Shaff is up to his scrawny neck in it. There's money to be made, good money, doing it, both horses and cattle. But there's another end of the scale, remember. Many men and not a few women have been whipped when caught. The unlucky ones get hanged, drumhead trial and ooff!, lights out. Ranchers and the law take a dim view of such stealing. And often as not I bet the County Sheriff, the real one, looks the other way. He's just glad not to have to deal with it."

"Oh. Well. You're right. Forget that idea."

The two fell silent. Pondering. No mines, what next. Old Mrs. Cobbson was right, they had to choose what to do. Even if they didn't like the options.

"Yeah, the more we talk, the more I think I need to go to Abby. How about you Cow? Isn't it time to see your wife and family?"

"Yeah, Ben it is. To hell with trying to find a mining job. Let's do it."

BEN RECOLLECTED, SIPPING COFFEE IN NEDERLAND. HE remembered her filling him in on her life while he was searching, going from mine camp to mine camp.

She told him how, In Cripple Creek, the school year was done. Abby had closed up the school building for the summer. She would occasionally check on it like the day she heard. After her return she saw a telegram wedged into the door at home. Curious and excited, she opened it.

WILL BE SALIDA NEXT TUESDAY STOP PONCHA STATION
NOON STOP ADVISE STATION MASTER THERE IF YOU CANT
BE THERE STOP YR DEPORTEE

She handed the gram to her brother. As he scanned it she asked, heavily, "Salida? Poncha? Why should I have to go? Why not here, why won't he come to me?"

Lon smiled sadly. "Remember. Any deportee who shows his face in Cripple will be beaten or worse. Ben is taking a risk even being in Colorado. I wonder where he's been and what he's been doing."

"You're right. I'm so glad to hear I forgot. That was a one way ride he took, no doubt there. I can't wait to see him! If he wants to meet things must be alright. Or at least getting better."

Lon nodded. "Do you want me to go with you?"

"No, Lon. Thank you but this is between me and him. And it is only a few hour's ride with a few stops and changes. I'll be safe on the train."

"Well, alright. Remind him of our offer. He is more than welcome to come work with us. I'll talk to the Owner's Association so he's safe to come back. He can manage the Double I while you teach and I handle other projects."

The Double I was always on his mind.

He faced his sister. Hands on her shoulders, he looked her in the eye.

"Abby. You go meet your man and do what you need to do. All I ask is that we talk before you make any big decisions. I mean, we are not only business partners but you are my sister and... Alright?"

"Yes, sure Lon." She was already planning her trip and her future.

VIII

"WHAT SHALL WE DO WITH COBBSON'S HORSES?" COW LOVED the feel and smells of the train as it chuffed and rocked down the hill towards Salida from Poncha Pass. He crowded a window to look as the Arkansas River came into view.

"Next stop, Poncha Springs. Seven minutes." The conductor twirled his whistle as he walked the length of the car. "Poncha, Six minutes. Stop is scheduled to be four minutes long."

"Four minutes? How can we get our horses out of the car in four minutes?"

The conductor winked. "Four minutes is about how long it takes to move everything the passengers need. We have it down to a science!"

Ben nodded. "Thanks."

Looking at Cow, he responded. "We keep 'em. The horses, that is. They're not ours to sell, and Cobbson would have us for horse thieves if we try. We just keep 'em, and if we see stray or strange cattle we tell him. He's not paying us now anyway, so let's just keep on keepin' on."

They rounded a corner. "Well, there's Poncha. We're almost there!"

Ben watched another locomotive in the distance. It pulled a short makeup up the river. From its stack came a burst of steam, its whistle blowing as it neared the station. The train was on the track coming from Pueblo and Canon City. He wondered and hoped that Abby was aboard.

HER RIDE WAS ALL DOWNHILL. SHE SOMETIMES FORGOT THAT Cripple sat at about ten thousand feet above the seas. The going was not bad, in fact fairly stable and even. Abby figured the grade and was as smooth as a quickly built narrow gauge road could provide. She barely felt the rocking. There were a few unscheduled stops outside of Cripple, before switching trains at Canon City. Those stops didn't really register with her.

She was too excited to focus on the train's stops and lurches. If she had, she would have known that the engineer and conductor were being extra cautious. They slowed or stopped to check anything out of the ordinary—diggings along the road bed, loose looking rails, even a dead animal alongside the tracks.

She of all people knew the hazards. Not all that long ago there were what some called 'incidents'. That was a nice way to describe destruction and even intent to kill. Recently some hot blooded union miners from Cripple had derailed a train on this stretch. No deaths or serious injuries but many folks were shaken up. Some property—freight and rolling stock— was destroyed. That was a while before the platform bombing which ensnared Ben and got him deported.

Supposedly shipping the union miners out of town calmed things down. Cripple Creekers were told that the union, the Western Federation of Miners, had been defanged. Even so, there were men around who weren't above sabotaging a train. Even a train full of innocent passengers.

Abby knew all of this better than she had ever wanted to. After all, the man she was going to see was one who had to leave town, leave her. Today, now, she shoved political and labor issues away. Getting to Poncha—and they were near, almost there—and seeing Ben was the thing. She couldn't wait!

FROM PONCHA STATION, BEN WATCHED THE APPROACHING train, wondering at the turns his life had taken. He spoke what both men were thinking.

"Well, now we need to decide what's next."

"What's next is you see your Abby and I see my wife Suze. And family." Cow grinned. "Let's all meet, at least the four of us, tomorrow. Breakfast. Main Hotel, seven thirty or so?

"Sounds good, pardner. See ya then."

TEARS OF JOY HAD COME AND GONE. THEY WERE IN PRIVATE AT last, off the train platform and in a hotel room. "Oh Ben, it is so good to have you back. I have so missed you."

"Me too. Did your school year end alright?"

"Yes, but I have it easy. I'm not the one who got herded out of town. I am relieved that you look healthy. A little slimmer, but you look good. I was worried."

"Yeah, a few hunger pangs along the way, but I feel alright. Glad to be alive and free."

She nodded as he continued.

"And especially thank you for sending me funds. Literally a godsend!"

"Who is Frank Mack? Is that the man you rode in with?"

"No, that is Cow. Another deportee I fell in with. Frank Mack. That is me. Was me?

"Is? Was? Ben, what do you mean?

"Ben McNall got deported, right? 'Cause I was supposedly a WFM man in Cripple Creek, right? You know that my name went on a list and it got telegraphed to every mine owner and sheriff in the region."

"You really think so?"

"Yes. No doubt. So. Frank Mack came to be. I sometimes use that name. I keep my real name pretty close. Only give it if I have to and trust the person."

"Oh. That makes all kinds of sense. I never really thought about that. So Frank appears now and then, and so does Ben? That makes sense." She knew she was babbling but couldn't stop. "So, tell me, what have you been doing?"

Then she went on in before he could say a word. "Please don't tell me you're trying to get back on at a mine somewhere. Are you?" She smiled, trying to make light; after half a beat he grinned.

"Yeah, well. When we got shoved out at the border things happened. The Sheriff confronted us just off the train, said we could stay in Raton overnight then get the hell out. 'You are not welcome', he said. To make sure we heard, he put his hand on his revolver as he said it. So Cow and I did some day work on a farm outside of town. Hard work, even for a miner!"

He sat. "Then the farmer hired us supposedly to find and round up cattle. Some big wheel guy there near Raton. But the job was too cute. We heard rumors later that he was an operator, running cattle on both sides of the law or something."

"Cute? You on a horse?! I bet it was!"

Ben shook his head. "You know what I mean. It just didn't add up. The pay was high and the work was easy. And he hired us on the spot, probably figured we were easy marks. Something about it was off. Not sure but like I said, we think it was a rustling operation. Cow and I were supposed to 'find stray calves and cows'. We figured we were being set up as a distraction from the main efforts. Not sure."

"Oh Ben. Maybe he was setting you up to be caught with some calves and get arrested or worse."

"That occurred to us too."

She hugged him, so glad he was alright.

"So what did you do?"

"We worked our way north. For a while we kept up the pretense of looking for cattle. Never saw a one! Once or twice telegrammed him that we had nothing. Then we just kind of dropped out."

"Oh? Will he come after you?"

"Maybe. I doubt it. We have kept track and can show effort if need be. Worst he could do is take back his horses and guns. Which would be inconvenient but not that bad."

Ben shrugged. "About what to do: Find a job. Cow and I figured we'd tour other mine towns and see if maybe we could get hired. Went to Creede, and the sheriff barely let us off the train. Said no miners are welcome. In Creede! A backwater, has been silver mining camp."

He took a sip. "This is good wine. Thanks for bringing it."

"Well, this is a celebration, isn't it?"

He smiled. "Yes, it sure is! Anyway, after Creede, we tried Bonanza, just over the hill from here. Same reception. Didn't see the sheriff but we definitely were not welcome even there, another has been mine town. Can you imagine the reception we'd get in a real gold mining camp? So I— we, me and Cow, figured no future in mining. Not for us not now. In a few years maybe but not now. So why bother with a new name?"

"Well, good riddance to Frank. But, I have to wonder, what are we going to do?"

He was thrilled but troubled at 'we'.

"We? Abby, here in Colorado I—me, Cow, the others, we are practically on the run. Not lawbreakers but we bring trouble and are not welcome. We're sure not model citizens. For that matter, I will run, literally, if I see Pinkerton men coming."

No explanation needed. She knew that private detectives hired by the mine owners were watching. And she knew what they would do to keep the deportees away.

He went on. "Abby. I don't have money, or a job, or any real prospects. And I can't go near a mine right now to make money."

"So? What you gonna do, Ben? Curl up in the corner and sob?"

Taking a step back, she glared, hands on her hips.

"Ben. You we don't need to live in fear of the security thugs. With one word you can step out of that nightmare. You didn't even need to leave Cripple!

"That's not fair, Abby."

"You're right Ben. Cheap shot. But don't forget, you can come manage the Double I. With us, me and Lon. You can work into part ownership. We offered you that before you got on that damned train. I sure wish you had taken us up on it. We would be much better off, all of us."

"How is Lon? Is he recovering from getting shot?" He remembered Abby's brother getting caught up in the firefight at a community meeting after the explosion."

"Yes. He's doing fine, thanks for asking. He worries about you too. And he wondered—wonders—why you didn't take us up on the offer."

"Ab, I couldn't. Things were so hot there in Cripple that even if I had stayed the Owners Association wouldn't have let me do that."

"You're may be right about that. We should probably let things cool a little before you return. How about your brother in Denver, what's his name, Gale? Gronk?"

Ben laughed. "Gronk? Isn't that the sound a bull makes before he charges?"

That joke fell flat as cow plop. After a moment he nodded.

"Gace, that's his name. You know, I forgot about him with all the excitement and then boredom of the last weeks. My little brother George Armstrong Custer McNall. As a young un he couldn't stand any of those names and he took to answering to Gace. He's an ex silver miner himself. He's been through some of what I have. Probably knows how I feel."

"Ex miner, huh? So he found something else to do for work, sounds like. If little brother can do that, so can you."

Ben smiled. "Now he's in the horse business. Maybe I need to go see him in Denver. If I can avoid the pinks."

"Good plan. I'm going with you."

She held up her hands, blocking his objection. "Don't you even think it, McNall. Don't start. I have money. School is out and I am free for the summer at least. And Pinkertons won't look twice if it is you and me and we stay away from the mining camps. They certainly won't pay attention to a couple in Denver."

She stepped forward, arms out for a hug.

"Aren't we meeting your friend Cow and his wife for breakfast? Let's enjoy the evening..."

"GOOD MORNING, COW. THIS IS ABBY."

"Hello!" Casually pointing a hand at his companion, he smiled. "Meet Suze, my wife."

Ben smiled. "He talks about you a lot, Suze. Wanting to see his wife and family."

She nodded curtly before sipping a cup of coffee. "And it is about time he got to us. My goodness, we have traveled all over. At least it feels like ages since we were feeling comfortable and safe. Me and the kids, that is. We left Cripple the day after he was sent away. We left the house, furniture, the kitchenware and tools and linens and clothes and all of it. I am never going go back to that place."

The silence gathered, each thinking of their experience those few days as the prosperous mining camp tore itself apart.

Cow nodded mournfully. "I had no idea. Wasn't sure what might happen to us. Had my hands full on the train and afterwards. Never occurred to me she would up and leave town herself."

Suze looked incredulous. "Why would we stay in a town that treated you, and us, that way? We just gathered up a few pictures, deeds and bank records, the family bible, and packed one suitcase each. Fled. Went to my sister in Pueblo. Have been waiting since."

They sat and ordered. Abby waited a few seconds to let Suze continue. She silently studied the menu, then filled the silence.

"Ben and I are going to Denver. To see his brother and..."

Suze interrupted. "Denver? Why Denver—there are no gold mines there."

The men exchanged glances. Cow cleared his throat.

"Well, Suze, my days of gold mining are done. At least in Colorado, at least for now. Armed security men are watching for me and Ben and for every other man who got deported."

"You broke no law. What can he do if he spots you?"

Cow blanched at her question.

Ben suppressed a snort as he jumped in. "Suze, we're taking a chance even coming back to Colorado so soon. If either of us shows up in a gold camp right now the Pinkerton goons will be all over us. Literally. They would love to give him or me a beating at least, possibly worse. Best we could hope for is another free train ride to the border. More likely a trip to the morgue. No thank you."

Cow nodded. "So now we need to find some other way to live."

Nodding slowly, Suze had an idea. Something she had read came to mind.

"Cow! There is a tunnel being built over by Montrose. It is not a mine at all, but an irrigation diversion tunnel. From the Gunnison river to farmland near the town. I saw an article. They are looking for men with hardrock mining experience! We should look at that.

Cow nodded. "Yeah, I heard about that. Worth a look. Montrose huh? I'd like to see the article. But in all honesty, Suze, we need to look at other possibilities. Other work."

She nodded unhappily. "We need to talk about that, Cow. We need to talk."

Cow looked at Abby then grinned at Ben.

"A brother in Denver, huh? You've been holding out on me. Family, and you didn't tell me!"

"Yes, my younger brother. Gace McNall. He is in the horse business."

"Oh?"

"Yup. He's an ex silver man himself. So he has some idea what we're going through. Never got himself deported but he lived through the silver crash of '93. Got dumped on the street overnight, him and thousands of other silver hardrock men all over the west. No warning, not even a 'thank you'." He paused. "Hard to believe that is over ten years ago."

They all knew about the Panic of 1893. Banks and businesses failed. At about the same time the Government stopped its silver buying guarantee. It had been buying millions of ounces of silver every month to back the Dollar. When it stopped with little warning, mines across the west closed up. Thousands of silver miners were let go. Businesses in silver mining towns went bust. Aspen, Leadville, Carson City, Creede, Silverton and other towns dried up and almost disappeared.

Cow slowly smiled. "The horse business, huh? I bet he knows a lot of people in the business. I wonder if he knows about shading."

"No doubt he's heard of it, "Ben rasped. "I imagine he's heard of robbery, and forgery too. But no brother of mine would change brands on livestock. He's an honest broker, not a damn rustler."

He set his coffee cup down hard. "Who do you think you're talking to anyway, Cow? Don't you know me even yet?"

He paused, getting his temper down. "And the sooner you forget about that shading, my friend, the better. That is a ticket to nowhere. Most likely it'd give you a quick swing from a rope over a tree branch."

Cow spread his hands in a gesture of peace.

"Just talking. I'm sorry. I didn't mean to upset or accuse you or your brother." He smiled tentatively. After a moment Ben nodded.

"Apology accepted."

Abby and Suze watched this exchange wide eyed, exchanging worried looks. Suze spoke.

"I don't know what this shading is, Cow. It sounds, well, bad. Like poison to me. Listen to your friend. Whatever it is, stay away from it."

Cow hoped he hadn't ruined things. He went on.

"I know a man in Denver too. Not a brother but he knows my family. Piers Sawicki? Sawinski? No, the name is Sawicki. I do remember that he goes by Paul. Maybe we'll ride up with you, meet him. I hear he has several businesses and maybe has jobs."

He glanced at his wife. "And Suze and I, we'll see what we see."

In a Nederland cafe, years later. Ben shook his head to clear old memories. His coffee had gone cold. His head was crowded. Meeting Abby in Poncha and deciding how to move on was a big deal. But it was time to forget all that. He had plenty to do in the here and now.

He looked out over the town. There was a storm working up, pushing around some snowflakes. Not a blizzard, just a heavy flurry. Everyone in town knew those flakes would be blown to in Kansas in a few hours.

He signaled to the waitress for another cup of coffee, and turned to his friend. "George, I'm concerned about the power lines to the mine. Need to have them checked before snow really starts to fly."

IX

GEORGE SET HIS CUP DOWN AND LOOKED AT BEN. "ARE YOU alright? Looks like you have been wool gathering."

"Yeah, old memories. Thinking on old friends and how Abby and I got from Cripple to Denver to here in Ned."

His friend glanced around to see who if anyone was listening in. "Say, sorry to intrude on fond memories. But we ought to talk. I have something you need to hear."

"Oh? I was wool gathering like you said. It is just that I saw an old name and it brought back memories. That's all. You have news? Let's hear it. Fire away."

George looked sharply at him, nodded, then leaned in.

"You know that black residue from the gold ore that everybody in town has? The stuff that appears with the gold ore that we have been washing away as dross?"

"Yeah. That stuff is a danged nuisance. Wish it would go away. What about it?"

In a taut, excited voice he went on. "Well, Ben, its not what we think, just gooey black stuff. Remember, you finally had me take some of it to be analyzed, assayed. Told the chemist to get to it when he could and it took a while. Truth be told, I wasn't expecting too much of it all. But guess what it is?"

"Just black sand. Ground up obsidian or something like that. Just black goop gumming up our works."

George smiled. "That 'goop' is tungsten, or to be precise, wolframite."

Ben wondered at his friend's excitement.

"Tungsten and wolfermite? What? What might a wolf do with that stuff?"

"Har har. Wolf-ra-mite and tungsten—the ore and the metal. Minerals. Usable stuff."

"Oh? If not gold or silver why do we want it? Them? Why not just keep washing it away?"

"Well Ben, they are useless if you let them just sit on the mine dump, gumming things up. Here's the thing: By itself, a lump of wolframite or if refined to tungsten, is just a paper weight. But."

Here Mason sat back, crossed his ankles, and paused.

"But. People want the stuff. Tungsten can be used to treat other metals. Alloyed with steel, it makes the steel harder and more durable. Done right, it can make steel much longer lasting, tougher, stronger. Can pretty much make it bullet proof, I understand."

He was talking faster and more excitedly. Ben tried to yank the reins.

"Bullet proof? George, have you been reading dime novels again?"

"No seriously Ben. Tungsten really does harden steel. Have you heard of Krupp?"

"Sure. Krupp and Company, a family owned outfit. Big German steel manufacturers. Steel for guns, bridges, battleships, and so forth. Again, so what?"

George nodded.

"Yup. I heard from a good source..."

Ben knew George was sweet on the woman running the hotel, very sweet. She knew when people came to town. If you wanted to know who was doing what, she was the one to go to. They talked, she and George, so Ben paid attention when he cited 'a good source'.

He went on "I guess the Krupp people are in Denver. Coming to Nederland Colorado! They have said they will take all of that black sludge they can get. You know that the boys from Pittsburgh and Cleveland and Chicago won't be far behind! 'Course they'll all pay more for refined concentrate than black sludge, but that's no surprise."

The big man sat back, hands locked behind his head, looking for all the world like a fleshy power pole or something. Ben had to laugh as George giggled and blurted.

"What this all means is, big orders for crud we've been flushing downstream, that's what!"

Ben thought quick. "So. I guess there is a bright side to the naval armament race, all those countries... Britain, Germany, Japan, the US, France, Italy, Russia. Seems like everybody is building more and bigger ships. And they'll all need steel, hard steel!"

"Not to mention artillery and other weapons. Hell, maybe even cavalry sabers. There's always demand for killing equipment, sorry to say."

"Yeah, unfortunate fact. But not only that. Plows and locomotives and buildings and automobiles and bicycles and aeroplanes. They all use steel too." He swigged his coffee which was not tasty at room temperature.

Ben set the coffee cup down.

"Say, George. That sludge comes from many, maybe most of the mines around the district. Some are active and some are abandoned or idle, open but just not working at present."

"True that."

"So, what I'm getting at is, are there other claims we can make or take over?"

Neither spoke for a moment. Each was looking the district over in their mind, running through claims and mines.

George spoke first. "I think we need to make a plan."

Ben looked out the window, talking low and slow. "I don't want to go hog wild here but this looks to be is a real opportunity. Who else knows about this, about the assay report?"

"No one. And I dropped a ten dollar bill on the assayer to keep it quiet."

"He probably would have anyway. But keeping a lid on this with a tenner was a good idea, George. Nice job."

"Don't know about other claims or mines or whatever, Ben. But let me poke around a little, quiet like. When I get the lay of things we'll talk, alright?"

George swilled his cold coffee, not at all daintily this time, and walked out, practically skipping with excitement.

Ben shoved his coffee aside. One bite of the cold and gooey short stack was enough. He didn't mind. He threw a dollar bill on the table and left. He imagined a map of the many old mining properties in the area. And all that fine black sandy mineral laying on and around them. George Mason's sludge. Who would have thought...?

He was ready to head home and share the news but remembered that the house was empty. Abby had mentioned she would spend the day in Denver. She was going to see her brother Lon and his family. It was a day of cousin time for their twins.

Ben wanted to share the news, get her take on it. Maybe he would make a telephone call. That'd take some planning since there were few sets in town, none at home. He'd have to go to a hotel or the general store. Nah, he thought, the owners often listened in. And they loved to gossip. No way, he decided. Making a call would get word out faster than an announcement in the newspaper. It would have to wait.

The wind hadn't let up. Ben shook his head, clearing visions of black sludge and thinking of mine operations. He got in the car, wishing it weren't so breezy inside the cab. He hoped that someone would invent a way to heat it for the driver and riders. Almost better to have saddled his horse up—no colder to do that than ride in automobile. He shivered most of the way up to the Deportati.

As expected, operations were in hand. Power was steady, the crew was working and ore was coming out with no problems. He poured a cup of coffee from the pot sitting on the little woodburner stove. Sat, thinking on how to maximize the tungsten opportunity. Shoving that daydream aside he worried how sturdy and dependable the power lines were.

The foreman came in, stomping his feet and crossed his arms, rubbing them as if cold. The crew were him and two others. He was senior and supervised; he liked to be called the foreman. Ben figured it did no harm. And it encouraged the guy's loyalty and work ethic.

The man poured himself a cup of joe, sat across from Ben. "Wind is picking up. Looks like our first storm is building."

Nodding, Ben kidded. "Yup, old Boreas is huffing and puffing today." The Norse god of the North Winds was practically a citizen of Nederland.

"Between you and me, I may be interested in picking up some old or inactive claim properties." Ben looked him in the eye. "But like I say, between you and me. Keep that to yourself. I'm telling you 'cause I want you to keep your eyes open. If you hear of or see an inactive claim that becomes available, let me know."

"Oh? Sure, I'll do that. What's up?"

"Looking to expand. You know that nuisance black sludge?"

"Yup. Pain in the keester."

"Well, it may be something that people will buy."

"Really!?"

"Seems to be the case. So, I am interested in acquiring properties we can get it from. But like I say, you keep that under your hat, you hear me? And stop washing it down the creek. We need to gather it. You be thinking about that and I'll round up some buyers."

"Sure Boss." He made a hand motion across his lips. "See, my mouth is sealed." He smiled as he stood and set the coffee cup down. "Better get back—got work to do. See you later."

<hr />

BEN NODDED, SAT BACK. FOR SOME REASON MEMORIES WERE strong this day. Thoughts of tungsten and power lines fell away. They took a back seat to his and Abby's trek from being near refugees to successful mine owners.

<hr />

Memories. Years back he was at Poncha Springs and the train coming in marked a watershed, a day his life pivoted in a new direction.

Ben and Cow's partnership was fraying. Both felt it. They kind of disliked that it was happening but recognized that times change. The old partnership wasn't needed now that they were off the road. It was time to go home, to recalibrate. To restart their lives. Both were so glad to see their loved ones.

They all decided the whole group would go to Denver. From there, they weren't sure, but for now, Abby and Ben would see Gace, Cow with Suze and their kids would see his friend Paul.

On the train later that day Abby looked out as they chugged north. The Colorado Springs station receded, Pikes Peak looming over it all. Briefly she thought of Lon in Cripple, southwest of the big peak. Thoughts gathered, she faced Ben, smiled, took his hand.

"You are gun shy right now about mining. Literally and figuratively. You of all people have good reasons to avoid the business. But remember, there is more to life than mucking ore at the bottom of a shaft for a few bucks a day. You are talented and can do well doing something else."

"You think so? Well, I have to say, right now I want to explore that 'more to life' you talk about."

"Of course. But remember. The Double I. A good, steady paying property near Cripple. Owned by yours truly."

He nodded, knowing where she was going with this. Her eyes were big and frank and she spoke clearly.

"Our offer stands. You come back to Cripple and manage operations. We have a formal agreement for you to work into part ownership. Cripple Creek Mine Owners Association and their lists be damned. We need someone to take the day to day oversight. Lon is looking at other opportunities and I have the school to look after. Those take time and energy, you know that. Having someone we trust running that mine would be a load off both our minds."

The phrase 'other opportunities' jumped at Ben.

"Other opportunities, that's what I want. What opportunities is he looking at?"

"I'm not sure, Ben. He has mentioned a lot of possibilities. Ranching, another mine, a hardware store. Maybe even a saloon. It seems to him that a liquor license is really a license to print money."

Chuckling, he agreed. "Yeah, they bring in good money. But those saloonkeepers earn it. Refereeing among drunk miners all day until closing at midnight or two in the morning. Clean and repair damage from fights after closing, and get supplies restocked. No thanks."

The silence between them lingered.

Ben nervously cleared his throat. "Speaking of the future, Abby. Our future. Do you want to keep teaching there in Cripple?"

"I would like to, yes. But not if you go somewhere else."

"The future is open, Ab. We can invent ourselves however and wherever we want."

"Do you want to stay in mining Ben?"

"As to the Double I. I can't be sure right now. Can't decide. In the mean time you two ought to look at other men, or you, for the job."

"You didn't answer. Do you want to stay in mining?"

"Not if I have to dodge security thugs all the time. I just don't know, Ab. I love working on and in the earth. Love the camaraderie. Love the risk, and the reward. Breaking out a day's worth of ore is satisfying and certainly is something to be proud of. Finding a chamber full of gold, even a small one, is exotic and exciting and a privilege."

He paused, thinking. "But... who needs to die in a cave in, or worse, a shootout between union goons and owners' thugs? Maybe this is the perfect time to look around. Does Lon want help with a ranch or maybe that hardware store?"

"Ben. Wherever you go, I go. Miner, storekeeper, blacksmith, opera singer. Whatever you do. I'd like to make it formal and get married. But I won't insist on it."

"Married? Whoa Nelly!" Ben was thrilled and somehow not surprised.

Smiling, eyes deep as the ocean, she nodded. "I'm Abby, not Nelly. Ben, let's us find a justice of the peace and marry."

He grinned. "I want to be with you too, Ab. But let's think this through."

"What's to think?"

"Are you sure you don't want to tell Lon? Have a traditional wedding? Won't he be hurt if you—we—surprise him like that? He's not only family, he is your, and likely my future, business partner."

She shrugged.

"Not only that, but let me ask you again. Are you sure you want to throw in with an unemployed, blackballed miner?"

"Ben. You don't have to be blackballed. Even if you don't want the Double I. There are other mines and related jobs. Let's us, you and me, look around. Maybe we can find an opportunity. There has to be some way, some place, to file a claim or better yet, buy a working mine."

ACROSS THE AISLE SUZE AND COW WERE TRYING TO DISCUSS their future. And present.

He glared at their offspring, raising cain in the seat behind them. "You three kids simmer down! Your mom and I are talking. Sit down, stop whining. Read a book or count the cattle we go by, or something. If you get noisy again, I'll give you something to whine about."

His threat and hard look brought a semblance of quiet and good behavior. Nodding, he turned to her as she spoke.

"The children have missed you. I have missed you. What are we going to do, Cow? Where will we live, how will we survive?"

"Well, we know it won't be gold mining. At least not here in Colorado."

"But you know so much about it. Are there other things you can do, like work on that irrigation tunnel? Or other big projects? New York City is tunneling to make a rail network below the city. A subway, they call it. Other cities too. If not, do you want to run a store in some mining towns?"

"Going back to a gold mining town now is out. Pinkerton and other thugs would love to get their hands on me. It'll have to be something else."

He shrugged, thinking. "I don't know. Right now I'll just hug the kids." He got up, went back and scooched in with his three children.

Suze picked up the newspaper she bought at one of the stops. On the front page was an article about coal mining in Boulder County, north of Denver. New seams were being found, mines opened, men being hired. And union reps coming to town to form locals. Oh joy, she thought.

"Cow, look at this." He returned, sat, studied the paper.

"Hmmm. Mining in or near a university town. What do you know!? The place may be worthwhile. At least the gold mine owners won't stink up the place. We'll have to see who owns them, I guess."

"LITTLETON COLORADO, FOUR MINUTES!"

The conductor glanced and saw the paper. He stopped, smiled. "Yup, that Boulder coalfield is a goin' Jenny." Hearing that expression brought Cow an image of Creede and Ben's description and how they agreed Jenny had left town.

The conductor of course kept talking. "My brother is opening a mine there and he is crying for good experienced people. Boom times!" He chuckled. "It is a hiring boom to make more mining booms!"

Turning, he again started down the aisle. "Littleton Colorado three minutes! Denver Union Station, twenty four minutes!"

Suze and Cow smiled as he shook the paper, pointing at the article.

"This is, I think, worth a look. But first I want to meet with Paul in Denver. I sent him a quick 'gram and asked to meet this afternoon. I expect he always has a lot of irons in the fire and maybe he can help us. Or maybe he can offer me a job."

Denver, later in the day.

A well dressed man sat alone in the restaurant. He looked out at Union Station and the bustle of comings and goings. Piers Sawicki savored his coffee. A telegram lay folded next to the saucer. He again looked at the telegram.

> Kicked out Cripple stop Coming Denver afternoon train stop Need to talk Ajax Café 4pm today stop C O Weston the third

Before coming west, Sawicki had adopted a new persona: Paul Sawyer. He learned early that in most places off the east coast a name like Piers Sawicki at the very least raised eyebrows. It caused some look down their noses. A few even asked if he spoke English! He shook his head wryly thinking of that. Hell, his line had been this side of the Atlantic for generations. Sawicki ancestors—his grandfather and some great uncles—had endured the cruel winter at Valley Forge. Speak English indeed!

But the man didn't bother to explain. Path of least resistance and all. He simply reinvented himself, taking the bland English sounding name.

No one in Denver knew it but he owed his start to a Weston. A favor given and a small loan in another time, another place. In fact his benefactor back in the day was also

C. O. Weston. Likely he was the father or maybe grandfather of the C. O. Weston who had sent the telegram. At least Paul was pretty sure of it.

The first time he read it, the last two words made Paul pay attention. He owed on the favor, needed to pay it forward. For that reason he was willing to meet the man, take his measure. Plus, he was curious what the guy wanted to talk about.

The clock said the three thirty train was due and he heard its whistle. Soon two couples, one with three children in tow, entered the café. The women were better dressed than the men.

"Paul?" One of the men approached and held out his hand. "I'm Weston, Charles Orville. Call me Cow. I think you knew my father."

Sawyer recognized the man.

"Yes, yes I did. When we last talked you were just entering university. Nice to see you again." He glanced at the others. Cow made introductions.

Coffee was ordered around, lemonade for the young ones. A little small talk around kids and wives.

Cow hesitated, plunged in.

"Let me cut to the quick, Paul. We" here Cow glanced at Ben "We were deported from Cripple Creek not long ago."

"Ah. Union men?"

"Sympathizers, not rowdies or goons. All we ask is fair pay for a day's work."

The other man shifted. "I am a dues paying member."

Cow ignored him and went on. "There are some union crazies. They shoot, derail trains, and blow up innocents. Thank God there are just a few of them, but it is not us."

"Well, that's good I guess. So what now?"

"Well, Paul, that's the thing. We are gold miners but the owners have made getting another gold mining job impossible."

Paul looked at them calculatedly. "Ah, yes, there has been a lot of press about that melee between miners, mine owners and the union. It is simmering across the west and just recently came to a boil in Cripple Creek."

Ben stepped in. "We're at a crossroads. We four talked, and Cow and Suze wanted to meet you. Wanted to get advice on where to go from here. He and I have been through tough times and a few adventures. Abby and I were coming to Denver anyway, so we thought we'd listen in."

After a pause he finished. "We're all thinking that this might be the time to make a change."

Suze took Cow's hand. "We're not sure. Maybe we, or he, will stay in mining. At least I want him to look into it. We hear there are coal mines in the Boulder area. And that they are hiring."

Cow gazed at her, looked over at Paul. "That is certainly worth considering. But mining is tough and dangerous. That's just talking work down the hole. Add to that the owners and their goons. Not sure it makes sense to step back into that cauldron."

He faced the businessman. "What about other opportunities—non mining work?"

Before Paul could respond, Ben spoke.

"I have a brother here in town, a successful horse trader. Gace McNall, you may know him. Abby and I will go see him soon. But your thoughts and advice are, like Cow says, welcome."

Paul looked around the table, directly to the eyes of the adults. Then, not saying a word, he reached into a vest pocket. Out came an old coin and of all things a jeweler's loupe. Ignoring them, loupe to his eye, the coin got a proper scrutiny. Turned to and fro, each side several times got the looksee. He did this for almost a minute. Back to the pocket went coin and glass.

He blinked, shook his head a little to clear it.

"Gace McNall. Good man, well connected and known."

Even as Sawyer spoke he regretted saying this. McNall was in fact well thought of. But Sawyer knew for a fact that his own reputation was, well, checkered. He really preferred his name not be brought up with Gace. Too late, he let it go. He smiled at Abby then Gace and was glad to see the couple stand, ready to leave.

"Thank you, Mr. Sawyer. I'll give your hello to Gace."

Sawyer simply nodded as he shook hands with them. "Good luck."

After they left, he again pulled out the loupe and twiddled it, clearly thinking. He stopped, smiled at Suze and Cow.

"Let me give this some thought. I know a man. In or around mining, not a hard rock man himself. He has connections down south, and up here. More to the point, he runs packing yards at many mining camps. Someone has to feed all those miners and their towns. That may be of interest to you—he will hire good men. Let me do some checking. In the mean time you might want to look into the Boulder County coal mines."

"Thank you, Paul. I will give your hello to my father next time I write."

As Paul nodded and shook hands he had a thought. "Say, there is one thing. I have a small company. Trading in mining claims. No hands on work, no mucking or drilling. I need someone with experience in mining, filing claims, and recognizing what's what in mining camps. What do you think of that?"

Cow paused. "So you have work in the mining business. But its all above ground. No cave ins or inhaling dust for hours? No thugs to dodge and no obnoxious owners to answer to? Yes, I'd like to know more."

Out came the loupe. It was brass and shiny from all the handling and twiddling. This time Paul waited only a breath before talking.

"Suze, describing this job will be boring technical talk. We'll drone on about corners and assays and overlaps and orphans and other mining terms and items."

He smiled, a crocodile smile that both attracted and unnerved her. "Perhaps we should let you two get settled where you want to live. Then Cow and I can talk business.

It struck her that Paul had taken control of their situation. Resentment swelled. Then she remembered the uncertainty and danger around the Cripple Creek explosion. And Cow's deportation and their penury and separation. The hard feeling was replaced by relief and gratitude. Glancing at Cow she saw he hadn't picked up on this.

Suze decided that it was actually a good thing to be taken care of. How nice for a change for someone to step in and take charge, to make the decisions and plans. And offer Cow a good job. That meant she and the children would have some peace and security.

"Why thank you Paul. Cow and I will find lodging and settle the children. You and he can talk tomorrow or the next day." She held out her arm for Cow to take and the left the office.

"Gosh, Suze, I thought you wanted me to go back to mining. Why the sudden change?"

X

"WHY THE SUDDEN CHANGE?"

Suze stopped on the sidewalk, faced her husband. "Cow. Your father knows this Paul Sawyer. The man is clearly well known and connected. You are on the run from a job and you have a family to support. This old family friend has offered you a mining job that isn't mining."

She paused, looking him in the eye, then smiled.

"Don't you see that this is the best of both worlds? The children and I get to live in a proper city. No more dumpy mining town with bullets flying. You get to use your mining experience. And don't have to risk your life in a shaft or get filthy or get deported. And you need to ask him but my guess is, it will pay better than working down in the mine."

He blinked, nodded. "Ah. Well. You have a point. I will talk with him again. No promises but let's see about it. It would be nice not to have to worry about you. Not to mention me dodging the pinks. Now, where do you want to live? What features do you want in a place to live?"

He didn't expect her random thought and question. "Ben's brother is Gace? What an unusual name! Do you know about that?"

"I guess he didn't like his full name, George Armstrong Custer McNall. Understandably so. At age three or so he came up with Gace and would answer only to that. So that's the story!"

"Oh. How interesting." Her expression said she thought it was anything but, and she came back to their situation. "I want a house near the trolley line. With shopping and a school nearby."

Cow nodded. "Let's go see what we can find."

A FEW MINUTES BEFORE THIS, WHEN HE AND ABBY GOT TO THE street, Ben fished in his pocket and took out a note from Gace. He held it out to a passing policeman.

"How do we get to this place? Can we walk or should we hire a cab?"

The cop looked them over, quickly but piercingly.

"Are you a miner? We don't want trouble here in Denver."

Taken aback, Ben paused. "I have worked as a miner, yes. But we are going to visit my brother. And we want trouble no more than you do, officer."

"Your brother, huh? Well, alright. Keep your nose clean." Then he broke into a smile, explained and pointed. They started walking.

She scowled. "Wow, the long arm of the Cripple Creek Mine Owners."

"Yeah, well, some of the enforcers they brought in to Cripple were Denver cops. Some just fired, some on leave. No love lost there. He may have seen me sometime or been told to be on watch for miners. Apparently he developed an eye for fleeing miners, or he remembered me. Or you."

"Me?!"

"Yes you. You are the teacher. Everyone knows and recognizes the town's teacher." He eyed her. "Especially a young attractive woman."

She blushed, elbowed him.

He went on. "Don't forget, Abby. You were seen at the protest meetings, sometimes talking or asking questions. And you were at the Victor open air meeting after the explosion when Lon and others got shot. And you were at the station when I got sent away. Lots of pinks and MOA men were watching that day. What, did you think they weren't watching community members too?"

She shook her head, a little shaken and concerned. "Well, we're in Denver now. We're minding our own business, going to see family. Let's go meet this Gace character."

Ben gawked a little at the big city's crowds and energy. "It has been quite a while since I was in a city like Denver. I bet there are plenty of ways to make money here. Paul said there were 'opportunities'. Wonder what he meant by that."

Abby kind of frowned. "I don't know, Ben. He seemed aloof, almost eely. Tread carefully.

"Eely? What the heck is that?"

"Slippery, oily, full of ulterior motives. He is in it for Paul no one else. And he will use people to get what Paul wants. At least that was my impression. The way he gave us the fisheye caused me chills. And he did that several times. Makes me wonder. Do you think he is on the up and up? And how did he know Cow's father?"

"He's different, I agree. What was with that jeweler's loupe? I figured he was just buying time to think. If I can I'll ask Cow about the connection."

They walked on, enjoying the freedom to explore their future.

"Anyway, Abby, I'm not sure I want to get in the horse business with my little brother. We'll see what he has to say. He may know Paul, or know of him."

"I still think we should find a JP."

"Really. You are bound and determined to tie up with an unemployed miner with limited prospects. Are you sure?!"

She stopped. "What, I'm not good enough? Why won't you give me a yes or no?'

"Abigail." He stopped too, faced her. "Yes, I want to be with you. And I treasure you being with me. But I want to know I can put food on the table. At least have some plan for it."

"I can understand that. But you can't get rid of me—I am going where you go, Benjamin Franklin McNall."

His smile confirmed what he said. "Good. Now we just need a way to live."

Street signs and numbers told the story. "We're almost there. You'll like Gace."

They entered an office area. A man sat, booted feet up on a desk, Stetson laying square on the middle of it, arms behind his head, eyes closed.

"I'm not buying today." He opened up and his eyes got big.

"Ben! I'm sorry, I thought you were my neighborhood magazine seller."

He came around the desk and they shook hands, looked each other over, and hugged.

"Gace, this is Abby."

"Hello Abby, nice to meet you." He nodded but resisted the urge to reach out.

He turned back to Ben. "I've been worried about you, big brother. Cripple Creek seemed ready to boil over all winter and spring. Were you caught up in that madness?"

"Yes. I got put on a train and sent to New Mexico. Just over the border."

"He was loaded up at bayonet point like cattle and deported, is what he is saying!" Abby sat heavily. "He has been on the run since the platform explosion. It is just a few days ago that I caught up with him. Now he's an ex-miner, like it or not."

Gace marveled that a woman like this was chasing—or chased by?—his brother. How did he get her in a man heavy mining camp like Cripple?

"Well I am glad you are alright. What have you been on the run from?" He had a good idea of it but wanted to hear from him.

"The mine owners' goons. Mr. Hamlin's goons. Pinks. Hamlin is a nabob in the mine owners' group. He keeps a list of non union men. Have to be on it to get a job at their mines. The mine owners have 'private eyes' aplenty. They're all over the state…"

Abby snorted. "Private eyes my aching back. They are thugs and goons and riffraff. And cops, like the one we just met."

Ben continued. "… making sure people like me don't get back into mining. If I went near a gold camp they'd be at me like slime on a fish. And I might not walk away."

"Ah. Where are you putting up? You two had better come stay with me for a while."

"We can't ask that."

"I'm telling, not asking. You two are staying. No ifs ands or buts." He looked from one to the other. They exchanged glances and both nodded.

He spoke. "Alright, Gace. Abby and I thank you."

Gace nodded in turn, and a wicked smile came over him. "And as to your 'private eyes'," here he fingered air quotes, "I'll tell a few friends. Ranchers and horsemen don't take kindly to Pinkerton men interfering with peaceable folks."

"Again, thank you." Abby stood and extended a hand to Gace.

A little taken aback, he shook it. "You are welcome."

Gace grabbed his hat. "Now. Let's go have a meal and catch up."

DISHES CLEARED, THE THREE WERE SAVORING COFFEE.

"This was the best and most relaxed meal I've had in days." Ben was full and it felt good not to have to look over his shoulder constantly. He felt a little drowsy but shook it off.

"Looking ahead, Gace. Here's a question. Do you know Paul Sawyer?"

"Short answer, yes. He's one I'd cross the road to avoid shaking his hand or talking to. How on earth did you run across him?"

"We just met him. I fell in with one of the deportees, on the train. His name is Cow Weston. We kind of watched each other's back on the train and worked our way north, to here. Anyway, Cow knew him, some family connection or something. We—me and Abby, Cow and his wife—met this morning for Cow to get advice. The two of us just sat in. Cow seemed taken by him. We're not sure."

Abby growled. "I think he's a snake oil salesman. Wouldn't trust him for the time of day."

"You called it, Abby." Gace paused, thinking. "I have never delved for the details, but there is talk, lots of it from quite a few folks. Some are gossips but some know what goes on in this city."

He looked around and spoke softly. "He was part of a mine scam. Salting the claim and booming shares to possible investors. It started to come apart somehow. Paul made to run away with the money and a woman. One of the women who set up the scheme. Apparently he intended to leave his wife and family. Story is, someone else got to the money first. After a day or two he had to retreat, tail between his legs, Wife took him back, people wonder why."

Gace stared away, eyes angry.

"The thing is, I hear he has picked up his business habits where he left off."

He took a mouthful of coffee, savoring it with full cheeks then swallowed. "Be careful. You didn't exactly ask, but if it were me, I'd stay away. He's trouble and more trouble."

Lightening up, he smiled. "And as long as I'm doling out advice, Ben, I'd say stay in mining."

Ben was surprised. "Oh?"

"Sure. Not down the hole moving ore or drilling for a shot. The thing is, you know enough to manage a property. That'd give you a good name. And take care of your Pinkerton problem. There have to be mines needing good management. Have you thought about that?"

Abby touched Ben's forearm, the cat eying the canary. With exaggerated innocence she cooed, "What a good idea Gace has! That *is* solid advice, isn't it, Ben?"

Ben shook his head in disbelief, looked between the two of them.

"Well, brother mine, Abby has been after me to do just that. Wants me to manage the Cripple Creek mine she and her brother own. Now you go and tell me the same thing." He laughed, not amused.

"How did you two plan this?"

"Hey, you know I have never laid eyes on her before today. But she knows the score, big brother. You ought to pay attention. Seriously, this is something you should take a hard look at."

Ben shrugged, met Abby's smiling gaze, and nodded thoughtfully.

"We'll see."

ACROSS TOWN THE NEXT MORNING THERE WAS A MEETING. Two old acquaintances touched swords as they negotiated an alliance. It was a hookup of convenience. Both kept an eye on the escape hatch.

Cow relaxed in Paul's office, catching up and making small talk.

"Suze found a house to rent, and got nested in for now. She and the kids like the set up. Not sure how long we will stay. It puts us in a good place for now. I have to say it is nicer than our place in Cripple. Plus there is so much more here in Denver. Saloons don't line the streets. There are churches, restaurants, schools, parks... This looks like it'll work out."

He stretched and stifled a yawn. "The coffee is good. It hits the spot since I missed breakfast this morning."

"I'm glad you're getting her and the family settled, Cow. You need to have your tribe safe and happy before you can to concentrate on the job."

"So, Paul. You mentioned some work. Mining without mining?"

"Yes. Work in the mine business without, like I said, moving rock and breathing dust."

"Yeah, I remember you said that. Doesn't add up on the face of it. Tell me what and where and how."

"Well, there are ways and ways. You have to use your imagination a bit, think differently and originally."

"Differently and originally?"

"Stick with me, Cow. Think about this: New mining claims are being filed all the time around a gold camp, no?"

"Oh yeah. Scores, even hundreds of 'em. Some well thought out and researched, some just a stab in the dark."

Paul nodded. "And overall, how many of those claims pan out?"

Cow smiled at the expression. Something that 'panned out' was a successful effort. A grizzled miner kneeling by the stream sloshing gravel in his gold pan knew the story real quick. If there was gold after he discarded the sand and gravel, it had 'panned out'.

"You know as well as I do. One or two hit it big and a few more become paying mines. Most are dry holes or the vein pinches out soon. No pay, lots of work and expense."

Paul nodded. "You hit the target dead on, Cow. Many, perhaps most, of those claims go nowhere. They are worked only slightly or not at all. Pretty quick it is clear there is no paying ore. So the claim is sold or more likely the miner just walks away. Abandoned."

"Yeah, I saw that a lot in Cripple and other camps."

Paul sat forward, intent. "And what happens to those claims?"

"Nothing. They sit. And grass grows over them."

Cow tried to think 'differently and originally'. An idea clicked and he blurted.

"Well, I suppose you could find a way to gain control of them. Somehow. Gain the rights to use or trade them."

Paul grinned, made a 'come on' motion with his hand and fingers.

Cow shrugged. "But who would want a stale, worthless mining claim?"

"Well, Cow. You have the idea. I buy up old, inactive, and abandoned claims. If you can find the old miner he is happy to get rid of it. They'll take pennies on the dollar. Some will sign it over for a bottle of whiskey. Often, the heirs will sign just to be done with it."

"So? Again, why bother? They're available precisely because they are worthless. They haven't panned out, to use your expression."

"You and I know that. But they may become valuable."

Cow scowled, shook his head, and gestured a 'how so?' with both hands.

"Think about it, Weston."

"I'm listening."

Paul grinned again. "If you buy up claims surrounding a good mine, you're ready to do lots of things. For starters, you can block your neighbor's growth. Or sell that mine's owners your nest of claims. So he can expand. Or sell to others to do as they will."

He paused. "You are limited only by your imagination. For example, you can sell your newly acquired old claims as 'valuable' to New York or London investors. As a potential new hit. After all, they are next to a hot property, aren't they? There are many ways to make them valuable in the buyer's eyes."

Cow nodded. "More valuable, huh?"

"Oh, Cow. Every claim out there has some asset, be it location or some little speck of ore or quartz hinting of ore or something. We find that little positive and play it up."

"And of course we sell the repackaged and fluffed up property as is, buyer beware and all."

"Yup. We can take a small investment—several hundred dollars. With the right promotion we can sell it for many thousands. Hell, more than once our new buyer has walked after a year or two. It has happened, not a lot but often enough, that we can buy the claim again for pennies."

Cow smiled. "So this is a way to mine without mining. What can you offer me to come aboard?"

Paul's cordiality dropped. He wasn't hostile, he was doing business.

"You know, Weston, or Cow as you want to be called, this is one hundred percent confidential. All we discuss or learn stays between us." He stared hard. "Do you understand and agree?"

Cow was a little taken aback by the change. "Yes, of course. This conversation is confidential, totally discreet. Just you and me."

Paul nodded. 'And you will sign a contract. I will give you an office and provide seed money. You go find and buy old claims. We will have several companies and partnerships and names to buy them under."

"So I would be buying in the name of several different companies and entities?"

"Yes. Cow, this is a good deal. The family connection you and I have is in play here. Your father helped me out once and I want to pass that on. So I offer you thirty percent of profits on deals you do."

"Thirty. Hmm."

Cow thought a moment.

"Alright. Here's another angle. Worth more and I will want fifty percent of the profit on these, whether I do the deal or someone else does." He went on, waiting for interruption. Belatedly he realized he should have pushed for thirty five or forty percent.

"Simple: buy up old claims around profitable mines. When the going mine touches one of our claims, we sue or threaten to send men in to stop them. If we play that right, they'll pay to get us out of their hair."

"Good approach, Cow. There have to be hundreds of mines like that." Paul knew he had been right to give Cow an opening. He smiled broadly. "Done, but you get fifty for your deals and a ten percent piece if someone else does the deal."

Cow was thinking there had to be a way to get railroad stocks in play. He mentally filed that away for another day.

They shook hands.

Paul cleared his throat, the pasted on a smile.

"Mr. Weston. One other thing, before you get going. Cow is certainly a unique name. But persuading people to invest, doing it so that they think it is their idea, is not easy. It calls for a certain... dignity. Isn't your name Carlton, like your father? Can we agree that you will use that when doing business? With the public, you're Carlton. You and me talking, Cow is fine. Do we see eye to eye on this?"

Cow didn't like being given orders but saw the sense of it. He shrugged.

"Alright. Frankly I don't want to be identified with him, my old man. Let's just say he and I don't agree on much. Do not mention him to any of our clients. And if you are in contact, do not mention me or that we are in business."

He turned the tables. "Do we see eye to eye on this?" He smiled, nodding. "I have to say, I see your point about the name. Carlton I am."

Paul nodded. "Good. Change of subject, again totally confidential. Another thing. I have varied business interests." He smirked. "Cow, think cattle." He stopped and Cow groaned on cue, then Paul continued.

"Cattle, horses, you name it. Always looking to grow the herd, if you know what I mean. In fact, I encourage my people to make that happen at every opportunity." His look was fraught with deceit, not saying what he meant. Cow thought he understood.

"Well now Paul. There are shades of meaning there."

Both knew that 'shading' was done by thieves—rustlers—looking to steal livestock. They shaded the brand, that is subtly changed it on the animal. Adding a bar or a 'C' or some small adjustment made a difference. It confused or outright changed who could claim ownership.

Cow continued. "I think I'd like that. Work on growing herds, that is, as well as the mining shares and claims. I'll work those angles, sure. Enough to say that I am in mining. But I have to say, I have developed a taste for being ahorse out riding the range. Not saying I won't work claims, just that I like being out in the field too."

"No reason you can't do both, Cow. Think on it."

They stood, the meeting over. "Well, I am going to get my wife settled. Will take a trip to the Boulder coal mines to make her happy, but that will likely go nowhere. If I am in mining, it'll be with you working the plans we discussed. So I'll go see her and get things straight. Then I'll get to work. See if I can make some money."

He extended his hand and they shook.

"And good luck to you, Carlton. Cow. Let me know if I can help."

XI

THE FLATIRON SHAPED CLIFFS JUST WEST OF TOWN DOMINATED. Cow and Suze approached Boulder uncertainly, just going to see what they could see.

Views unfolded as the train came over the hill. They saw dramatic mountains on one side, plains receding to the east.

"That mountainside is named well. It really does look like four or five flatirons are leaned up against it."

"Yes. And look at the one, third in from the right. A big 'CU' is painted on it."

Suze smiled. "Put there by Colorado University students with time on their hands, no doubt!"

They sat back, enjoying the sights, wondering what if anything the day had to offer.

As the engine nosed into the town, he stirred nervously then spoke.

"Suze. I don't want to mine. Even in a coal mining town it is risky for me. Maybe the pinks aren't looking for us here but maybe they are. So far they're lurking everywhere. I am just not ready to get back into it. Not just yet."

"Not yet? When? What will we do? How will we eat, where will we live?"

"We got us settled in Denver, didn't we?"

"Oh Cow, what do you want? Me, I just want a house we'll stay in, and for you to have a job."

"Well, Sawicki offered me a job."

"Sawicki? Who's that? I thought Paul's name was—is—Sawyer?"

"My dad knew him back east years ago and they did some business. In those days he went by Sawicki. I guess he has taken on a new name. He's Sawicki to me but I'll get used to Sawyer I imagine. Anyway, like I was saying, he offered a job. But I owe it to you, the family and myself to at least look around."

"I don't know, Cow. There are mining jobs going begging in Boulder County. It would be so easy."

"For you, yes. Not so much for me. It is hard work."

"You think running a house and keeping three kids is easy work?"

"Not saying that. You work hard and do it well. Anyone looking at the kids can see that, see your hard work. The thing is, security thugs are still looking for me and other gold miners."

She nodded, mollified.

"Yes, I forget that mining isn't easy work. And I don't want you to get marched on to a train again, sent away. I would die if that happens."

"Or I might, Suze. Don't downplay that. Here's the thing. Sa—Paul offered me a job. It is up in the sunshine. Some of it involves mining, but not mucking ore or planting charges. No work down the hole at all. And I'll be doing some other things too. It is a rare opportunity, best of both worlds. And I think I will like it and do well with it. It is for me, Suze. This is our chance to try something new. I don't want to be deported again either. Nor do I want to worry about miner's cough and cave-ins and all of that. This is different."

"Different? How? Can you provide for the children, feed and clothe them? Not to mention your wife?"

She shrugged, knowing she couldn't win this battle. If he didn't want to mine a team of horses couldn't drag him into one. Time to sidestep.

"Alright. Let's go on. I'll get the family settled. Where you put us in Denver is just fine. I will send for our furniture from Cripple. Don't you think we should at least try to sell the house there?"

"Yes, let's."

She nodded. "Alright. You go talk to your Sawyer or Sawicki or whoever he says he is about this job."

She gazed at the spectacular cliffs above the city. "Be careful with him, Cow. Don't you wonder what he is hiding with his new name?"

Cow snorted. "That's easy. Go back to kindergarten. Remember the kids who made fun of you or the poor kid in class almost no one liked?"

"Yeah? So?"

"He wants to be accepted. Look at his background and ancestry. Some folks don't like anyone with a funny last name. Around here, people with English sounding names can get things done. If your name ends in a vowel you're looked down on. By everyone, from the grocer's store to the downtown clubs."

She paused, nodded. "I guess so. Never really thought about it."

He kind of nodded. "That is, if with your multi syllable name, you can even get inside one of those gentlemen's fortresses. It is hard to build alliances and connections with folks who sneer at you. Believe me, I know. I fled the east to escape that rigid, class and background snobbery."

He sat back down. "Thanks, Suze. I'll take him up on that, the not a miner's job. Let's go back to Denver and get you into the place. Then I'll go get with Paul. It will be good for us, you watch and see."

Cow was glad he had some family backing. Not just Suze and the kids, which was important. He had some financial resources from his parents and ancestors.

Not that he had much moral support. To be precise, he had a trust account which he likely wouldn't outlive. Contact with his siblings and relatives had withered and he hadn't been back for years. But the account was securely paying out from a mutually agreed bank.

Moving the family furniture and other property and selling the house in Cripple took a few days. He had the help of a lawyer Paul set him up with. It finally looked like the family was settled and his wife was happy.

He looked forward to the meeting with Paul.

As Cow entered, Paul stood and extended his hand. Cow couldn't help but admire the view of Mount Evans to the west and the State Capitol building to the south.

"You really do have nice quarters here."

"Thanks. It took a while. Held out for this location, central with a view." He took a moment to enjoy the panorama, quiet and smiling.

"It is good to see your family is settled, Cow. At least I assume all is well with Suze and your children?"

"Yes, mama and kids are happy. Glad to have that done!"

"Good to hear. Tell me, have you thought on our conversation the other day?"

"Yes, and I'm ready to go with it."

Paul smiled. "Good. I have some folks you need to meet. Some mine owners, some lawyers, some ranchers and cattlemen."

He bellowed, "Forbes! Bring us coffee."

A tall skinny negro entered. He balanced a tray with coffee pot, two cups, and a plate of cookies.

"Just set them here please. Forbes, this is my friend Cow."

The assistant nodded at Cow, glanced at Paul and back to Cow. "Cow. Nice to meet you. If I can be of help, just let me know." He set his tray down, nodded, looked again at Paul then the visitor. "I'll moo-ve on."

Smirking, he eyed the guest and nodded. "Cow."

Paul guffawed. "I can't believe I pay you to hang around! You're lucky I can't a-forbes to pay some other helper more money!"

Forbes did a formal bow, chuckling, turned and left. Paul rolled his eyes. "Ya gotta laugh."

Taken aback by the informal offbeat humor, Cow took a sip of coffee. Made a mental note not to take himself too seriously. Then jumped in. "Thanks for the offer, mining claims and cattle work. Like I said, I look forward to working without having to go underground."

Paul gazed at him, a frown taking over from the puns and laughter.

"Weston. Can you keep eyes and ears open, and mouth shut?"

Surprised at the gruff change of subject, Cow hesitated. First thought was to say 'heck yes'. But the message came through. Doing just what Paul wanted, he nodded and watched.

Paul stared hard long enough to make Cow squirm. "You know, all those mining camps up in the mountains. There are thousands of men—and women—in towns and camps all around."

Cow arched his eyebrows and shrugged in agreement.

"They all eat. Ever wondered about that? Where food and supplies come from? How all that stuff gets to them?

"Ah…"

Sawyer talked over him. "And how about the money to back the stores and other businesses? Who provides that? How does a man wanting to start a store or work a claim get backing? Or a hostess wanting to work the miners?"

Cow sat looking at the man who, as a kid, he knew as Mr. Sawicki. Neither spoke for a minute or so.

It was safe to talk, Cow felt. "So, Paul Sawyer. You work to supply and feed these places. And finance them. How can we make it better and more profitable?"

Paul continued to gaze right through Cow. Cow half expected the loupe and a coin or gem of some kind to come out of a pocket. No, but the older man almost nodded before he spoke.

"Alright Carlton. Cow. You seem to get the program. We'll give you a try."

"Go home, be with mama and the kids. Get settled and rested. And, day after tomorrow, go to our stables. Forbes will give you the location. Early morning, at seven. Be ready for outdoor activity, horseback riding, living rough. If you want to bring a sidearm, fine, but no rifle or shotgun. Our horse not yours. You'll be gone for several days, maybe a week. If you have a trusted friend who can ride and knows how to keep quiet, bring him."

Sawyer paused, looking his man in the eye. "Outside of that, keep this conversation under your hat. Tell no one, not even Suze. Got that?"

Cow was uneasy not telling his wife. Wanting to do a good job, be part of the team, won out.

"Understood, Paul."

COW WAS THINKING ON HIS NEW ASSIGNMENT AS HE WENT TO meet Ben. Earlier they had agreed to meet over breakfast and get current.

"So how did you and your brother get along? Been a while since you'd seen him, no?" Cow speared and bit a chunk of sausage, looking at his friend.

Ben swallowed a mouthful of flapjacks, washing them down with coffee.

"It was, is, good to see him. Nice to reconnect, to catch up. He was a silver miner once. Unlike me he got out after the Crash of '93. Yeah, it has been years, too long. Hard to believe, but it has been quite a while."

He smiled. "Gace has offered me a little job for now. Helping him out in his livestock trading. It'll tide me over. At least until I figure out what to do next. You? What are you up to?"

Ben and Cow. Thrown together by circumstance, forced onto a train and exiled. They had to be close and trusting while riding the rails and then on the trail. That was then.

Being back with family and job concerns was in a way jarring. Not surprisingly, all of that was pulling them apart. Not that they distrusted each other. Just that now, they had priorities other than surviving the day and watching for pinks. Neither was inclined to spill about their personal future.

Back to reality.

"Oh? That's good. Yeah, Paul has offered me a job as well."

"Good for you. Is it in mining?"

"Not really, Ben, no. Not mining." His tone shut the door to further questions. Both realized he hadn't really answered the question.

Ben glanced at a clock on the restaurant wall.

"Well, I need to go. Have some things to get done." He stood.

"Take care, Cow. Hi to Suze and the kids. And you be careful out there, my friend."

They shook hands. Went their way.

THE WESTON FAMILY'S DAY WENT FAST. SOON ENOUGH IT WAS time to leave for the job. An early start. Suze fixed a breakfast as the kids slept.

"When will you be back, Cow?"

"Not sure. A few days, a week, depends."

"All you'll say is it is a job for Paul. That worries me. What is it?"

"I'm not sure. I know it will be outdoors." With this he looked down at his denims and riding boots. "This won't be a formal business meeting, that's for sure." He smiled. "I will tell you more when I can, love. See you soon."

PAUL MADE A BRIEF SHOW AS COW GOT HIS HORSE AND GEAR. He seemed to be in a hurry, dressed in coat and tie. He didn't even look his man in the eye.

"You stick with these men, Cow. And do what needs done. Like we talked, eyes and ears open, mouth shut."

He left without shaking Cow's hand and didn't look back.

They mounted up, Cow and others, and headed out.

XII

In the mountains somewhere west of Denver, a small campfire's flames danced and shone. The dawn's dark overwhelmed as it feebly tried to bring light.

"Hey man, time to get up. Drop your..." The cowboy who had spent several years in the US Navy stopped his dawn chant, remembering he was in the Rocky Mountains not at sea. "Get up and let's get goin'." Punctuated by a none too gentle foot nudge, the words opened Cow's eyes. For the rest of his life he would think of his waking angel as the Nudger.

He unrolled from the blanket, sat up. Shook his boots out and was happy to see no creepy crawlies tumble out. Pulled up his socks then the boots.

"I know you're new, Cow. Sawyer just put you on yesterday. A quick word: Don't let the boss see you doing that. If we have to get up and go quick to chase a herd or worse a horse, ya need to be ready. I tell ya, best to sleep in your boots, man. It'll save you. Putting boots on in a hurry in the dark when the herd is running is no fun, believe me. Sometimes we have to get up and go fast."

Cow was skeptical, but as the new guy he just nodded. "Is there coffee?"

Nudger grinned, gestured to the pot on the fire. There was also a curious set up. He saw several three foot metal rods stuck into the fire. They each had a three quarter circle handle on the cold end. Cow had seen one had a straight bar on the other end, and another a half circle, and another a capital L.

'Ah, those must be tools for shading,' he thought.

Nudger talked. "Yup. On the fire. But drink fast. Seems there's a herd just over the next hill. We need to go find us a calf or mamas and calves. Branding iron is heating as we jaw. Saddle up and let's go!"

They were three. Quietly, single file, they rode up over and halfway up another hill. The chief stopped. Maybe he wasn't a chief, just senior cowhand. Chief is what Cow named him, in his mind. No way would he say it out loud. Chief pointed to the other guy, to Nudger. "Go around, head them down valley. Back towards our fire. Cow will go and move 'em over this way. I will stop the herd, look 'em over. Then we'll take what we can. Go."

Nudger smiled, nodded. Then he reined his horse out and quietly left.

"You, Cow, you go the other way, stop so you can send the herd back towards me and the fire. Be quiet, don't gallop. Go."

Cow got to what he thought a good place to send the herd to the Chief. He backed his horse into a small stand of aspen trees. He figured it was good enough that the herd wouldn't see him and shy away. He was downwind too which made it that much better. Day was breaking. He saw some cattle meandering down towards him. And a man on a horse. He assumed it was Nudger pushing them his way.

No. It was not Nudger. It was someone else, different hat, different horse. Definitely not his guy. And then someone else jerkily rode up behind the guy. Two! What was happening? Where was his buddy the Nudger?

Cow sat quietly, trying to make sense of it. Looking over his shoulder, he saw an escape route. For the moment he remained and watched. Up the valley he saw two more horses—the Nudger, one hand on reins and the other in the air, and he seemed tense and glum. The rider behind him had a gun drawn, pointed at Cow's buddy riding who was in front!

Cow was breathing fast, and time was going very slow. Time to cha-cha, he thought. Get the hell out. This was out of control.

Then one of the first two men spurred his horse forward, apparently looking to head the cattle off. The others stayed put, still holding Nudger at gunpoint. Cow stared, ready to bolt but stuck, unable to move.

The man, the approaching rider, looked and rode like Ben. A friend! Or so he thought. As that desperate hope came to mind, he saw his friend Nudger pulled off his horse. One of the men shoved him to the ground and kicked. One held a gun on him and the other threw a rope over a tree branch. Cow felt he was seeing a show or a play in a mirror or something. None of it seemed real. Nudger raised hands in a plea.

For some reason Cow didn't scram. He couldn't move. His horse sensed the tension and was quiet and still. He pulled his horse a step out of the grove to get a look at the oncoming rider. The man stopped. He and Cow stared at each other across the meadow. It sure as hell could be Ben.

But that couldn't be! Ben was with Abby back in Denver! With his brother Gace!

Cow wheeled and fled.

THE TWO MEN COULDN'T MAKE THINGS ADD UP. BEN AND COW were looking in opposite ends of the telescope, seeing events that made sense but didn't make sense. Neither one ever dared do ask the other if he was there or what he saw.

A FEW DAYS AGO, COW WAS GETTING HIS ASSIGNMENT FROM Paul. At the same time, Ben and Gace struck a deal. It seemed that Gace owed a favor to a rancher friend. The friend needed a little help moving a herd. Not having a real job or anything, Ben got nominated and immediately elected for the 'little job'.

A few days later Ben found himself out riding on the range. And again he was reminded why he left the farm. Reliving the past few days, thinking and pondering, Ben just let the horse amble along. Not that he could get the nag to go faster anyway.

The rancher man and his family were Gace's friends and clients. 'Client' seemed over the top to Ben. Someone who bought horses was a just customer, seemed to him. But he kept quiet about it. Gace really did value the business they sent his way. So, Ben was cowboying for a week or so. As the new dude, got the oldest stubbornest horse on the place. Moving slow suited Ben anyway.

The 'little job' entailed living in the saddle for a few days. When not in the saddle, he was sleeping on the ground wrapped in a blanket. This morning at least he got a cup of coffee, some bacon, and a slab of bread with butter. The bread wasn't rock hard and the butter was sweet. He felt fortunate to have it. Certainly it was more of a meal than he and Cow had gotten after the train.

Ben's horse caught up with the rest of the crew who were waiting, horses munching meadow grass and the men quietly talking. Ben could have eaten more bread and butter but it was gone or packed up. No matter; it was time to get to work. He saw the boss, and the two other men. He called them—in his mind, not out loud, Chewer and Noisy. Ben was careful not to talk much, especially nicknames. He needed all the fun he could get, so turned those names and personalities over in his mind while riding slow.

They stopped talking as Ben pulled up. The boss spoke. "The herd is over that hill."

The rancher lifted his head, nodded to indicate which hill. His two hired hands like most hired cowpokes were characters. Intentionally or not, they lived large. One, Noisy, burped a lot. And he did it loud enough to make coyotes howl in response. That intrigued Ben, the inadvertent communication. Something else to ponder while riding slow, he figured. The other, Chewer, smacked and chewed, open mouthed. It was almost as if the bread was fighting back. Ben knew miners just as eccentric and took it all in stride. All four were focused on the herd now, and they looked that direction, ready to get to business.

"Finish up, tighten your rig, get ready. You" he pointed at Noisy "and Ben go get a look. Stop at the hill and hold for us. We'll decide what to do then. And be quiet. We're upwind and the herd might spook and run, which God knows we don't want!"

The two got to the top of the hill. The horses sensed the tension and seemed to pick footing with care.

"Looks about right. I didn't count here but last night we had forty two cows and calves." Noisy looked around. "Hey."

His tone was urgent and he pointed unobtrusively. "There's a man down in those aspen." Ben craned to look.

The rancher came up, followed by two men on horse. Chewer was caboose, bringing up the rear. And he held a pistol on the man in the middle! He spoke, roughly and loud.

"Look what we got us. A goddamn rustler! Had one of our calves down and knife out, ready to cut a notch in the ear to claim it."

The man Cow thought of as Nudger glared and his tongue ran away with him. "And I damn near got it done. You're lucky you saw me or your herd would be smaller." Soon as he said it he knew he was going to get the worst. He closed his eyes, thinking of his mama and his horse. He knew he was on the way out.

Noisy stared at him. "Our herd? Your herd? You piece of dog..." Looking at the rancher, he nodded downhill. "There's another one down there. We ought to go get him too."

"Ben, you go flush him out. Catch him if you can, at least run him off. We have some business here you needn't be part of."

Ben nodded, kicked the horse. It moved out, fast for its age, at a slow trot. The rancher watched him go. Then he got a length of rope out and nodded at the Chewer who got off, pulled the admitted rustler off the horse and kicked him. The rope went over a tree branch.

Ben heard voices being raised. He didn't want to know, didn't want to listen. He had a good idea of what was about to happen. He shut it out and concentrated on trotting his horse down the hill while trying not to spook the herd.

He stopped as he got within a long rock throw of where the man was. The other guy's horse stepped out of the aspen grove. The two riders' eyes locked and they froze. After a second or two the man wheeled and took off through the aspen.

Ben McNall was shaken. The guy looked familiar somehow. Good God, was it Cow? Nah, couldn't be, he was doing mining work for his friend Paul. His shady friend...

The horse got excited and took Ben after him. At least the nag tried to. Old and slow, it was no match. The guy was gone. No trace. Good enough that I ran him off, Ben decided. His mind churned: All he could think was, God I hope that wasn't who I think it was. He turned back up the hill, dreading what he would find.

The Rancher and Noisy met him halfway.

"You ran him off? Good. He'll tell his gang what happened to their pal. They'll move on. I hate to send them to easier pickings somewhere else. But we have a ranch to run."

The rancher glanced up the hill at the body swaying on a rope. "He was part of a gang been around for weeks now. They've been nipping bits and pieces of our herd and from neighbor ranches as well. The damn fool got what he asked for."

He took off his hat, wiped his brow, looked his men in the eye. "I hate this part of being a cattleman." Hat back on, he scoped his cattle. "Let's go. We have a herd to move."

That image of that body swinging on a rope was etched into Ben's soul, and probably the others' too. He for one would carry it to the grave. He decided then and there the cattle business was not for him.

Mining it was. And Abby. He wanted to get her to a JP quick. Get hitched!

And maybe, Ben decided, he would swallow his pride and go back to manage the Double I in Cripple. That or find and buy another property. Maybe Gace had some money. The rest of his family sure didn't. Possibly he should approach Lon and Abby. Lon wanted to diversify and maybe this was the time to do it. He knew there was a mining district west of Boulder, Nairalin or some name like that. Nederland, that was it. Hearsay was it had some opportunities. Maybe he and Abby could find something up there...

The grotesque memory of the body swinging off a tree would sometimes appear to disturb and upset. That day also gave recall of a friend gone wrong. That memory too would last, to bubble up unexpectedly.

YEARS LATER BEN FOUND HIMSELF A SUCCESSFUL NEDERLAND miner. Well, half owner of a mine, happily sleeping with the other owner. He sure was glad he and Abby had managed to raise money and buy their own property. They liked this part of the state. He thought to yesterday and George's word on the tungsten and all. That was exciting!

Today he had many things to keep in mind: ore and assays and mechanical equipment at the mine and so on. Thank goodness those cattle driving memories came rarely.

One task for the day was to make sure the mine would have power all winter. Last thing he wanted was an outage. That'd leave his men in the dark with no means to continue drilling or other work. Unsafe for them and bad for business. He would have to get that power line guy out to look things over. What was his name, Ted Moore? Eldorado Springs guy. Hopefully he could tell if the lines were ok for the power needed.

He drove slowly from the café in Nederland up to the Deportati. He made a vow then to come out in the spring and smooth the road. There were plenty of pot holes that needed filling. Bad enough now in the fall, they would be much worse by then. The wind moaned. Ben shook his head, concentrating on the mine.

Tungsten. The word bounced round inside his head. He hoped George was locking up all the claims he could. No doubt he'd do a fine job of it—he always did. Good thing, because when, not if, word got out, every New York investor would be here buying up properties. Important for us to nab the productive ones first. As many as we can. The thought occurred, maybe they could sell some of the deadbeat claims to those eastern investors. Or the claims they had already worked over. Another way to make money...

He imagined Abby's response to all of this. "Money gushing in won't be just innocent capital from New York. If there is such a thing. There are plenty of other miners looking to cash in. And don't forget the flimflammers. They'll be here like moths to a candle. We need to get in on the ground floor."

He stopped to look at a power pole. The northwest winds had worn that side of the pole smooth. He hoped it was strong enough to last the season. What was that guy's name? Moore. He had to get hold of Moore to survey his situation.

Then for some reason, maybe it was the cross bar on the power pole. He thought back to the lynching, and wondered what Cow did after that.

COW TOO WAS SCARRED, AND SOMETIMES UNWILLINGLY remembered that body's horrible motion. It was hard to relive but he couldn't completely stuff it away and forget. Seeing his partner and new pal being kicked and begging for life came to him less often over time, but still...

That day, that hour, Cow knew. He would go back full time to working mining stocks and claims. He wanted nothing to do with horses, cattle, ranching, or anything to do with livestock.

He would have to go talk with Paul.

It was a few days after his encounter with the ranchers, and Cow was still upset. When he got home he mentioned uprooting and moving away. Suze wouldn't hear of it. "We're just getting settled, and the furniture from the house in Cripple just arrived. We're staying right here, Cow Weston."

Cow didn't know but assumed that Paul was shaken by the loss of one of his men. Not to mention having to move his gang on somewhere and start over. At the meeting the boss didn't let on to being unhappy. Paul was not one to share the big picture.

Cow came straight out with it. "Running cattle for you isn't down my alley, Paul. I won't go out again to do that. I simply won't. Let's talk about those mining shares."

"Oh? Life in the saddle isn't for you, huh? Well, Carlton, there's plenty to do..."

Cow wasn't buying it. "Life in the saddle isn't bad, Sawicki. What gets me is the opposite. Death, sudden death by hanging. Your guy got caught messing around with another man's cattle. He paid the big price. For a calf or two, end up swinging? Hell no! That could have been me!" He stared at the older man. "Me!"

After a moment his tone softened. "Paul, I will not do that. Of course your position is you knew nothing about that work and so forth. Well, whatever you say. But I won't have it."

He looked Paul in the eye, and went on.

"Now, I don't mind finding old claims and filing new ones and getting investors to pony up one way or another. That is something I think I will do well. But I tell you, chasing cows—yours or someone else's—is out the window. No more, no way no how. You know what I mean."

So did Paul. "It is a risky business. I understand. No cows for Cow. From now on it is just paper for Carlton."

They shook hands.

"Alright. Carlton, how about you go to Central City. Take a look around."

"To follow my nose? Or is there something special to look for?"

"There are plenty of overlapping claims up there. Hundreds, maybe thousands of 'em. Maybe you can lasso a few of them and squeeze someone. Do you understand what I'm saying?"

"Loud and clear. I'll take the mid day train." On the way out he stopped. "I imagine I will find a played out property, or several. Maybe we can make something of it. What do you think?"

"Sure, Carlton. Just keep us in the mining claims business, not the ore moving business. Good luck!"

Carlton did just that for many trips. He did well connecting with old owners and new investors.

YEARS PASSED. MONEY ROLLED IN AND PROPERTY WAS ACQUIRED.

NEDERLAND IN THE EVENING. THE SIGH OF WIND, THE AFTER-glow on the mountains. A good time to assess the day, talk, connect. After the kids were in bed and quieting down, the couple talked.

"Abby. You know that sludge we've been dealing with? The waste from our gold processing?"

"You mean the black stuff that clogs the mills that we just dump down the tailings piles?"

"Yup. Get this. It isn't gummy worthless sludge. It is wolframite. Tungsten ore. Valuable in its own right."

"Oh? I wondered about that stuff."

"Yeah. George ran an assay. We think it is secret, at least for now. Now, get this—I'm told the Krupps are interested. That German family empire with mines and mills and foundries and artillery factories. They are looking for regular supplies of the stuff."

"Well, if they are you can bet that American steel producers are too. Why do they want it anyway?"

"It is used to harden steel. Battleship armor and the like."

"Ah. Plenty of demand for that worldwide. The Brits and the Germans are trying to one up each other with bigger battle ships. And Teddy Roosevelt has his 'Big White Fleet' and his 'Speak softly but carry a big stick' philosophy. In Russia the Tsar has just finished his Moscow to Siberia railroad, all five thousand miles of it. No doubt that took lots of iron and steel and probably your tungsten. And other railroads are laying track everywhere. This sludge could be a gold mine for us."

He groaned as she giggled and owned up. "So to speak."

"Here in Colorado. All the sugar beet farmers need plows and rakes and seeders and the sugar companies need steel for their refineries. The Pueblo steel mills... This wolframite could be a godsend."

Abby stood, walked to the window and looked out into the valley.

"You're right, word will get out if it hasn't already. How many claims around here can we get? To take the sludge, before others have that idea. I mean, sewed up, with full rights to 'em, fast?"

"I put George to doing that just this morning. Today he got signatures locking in three inactive properties around the Deportati. More on the way. We need to talk with ex miners and their heirs, up and down the valley."

"Good. I'll get out myself." She smiled, toothily enough to be a wolf. "You know, I'll be the poor helpless female looking for help and all that."

"God help the owners of the Nederland-Caribou District!"

XIII

COLORADO MINES HAD LONG BEEN DESIRABLE AND WIDELY traded properties. Every claim was filed with the expectation it would be a profitable source of gold, silver, and other minerals. And every filer hoped, dreamed that this mine would be 'the big one.'

After the initial working, a few claims hit big. Some gave respectable profits. Others—most of them—played out or never gave a dime of profit.

People acquire, trade, upgrade, downsize. There is always a market for these properties. New or old, no matter. Some are sought for access to mineral deposits. Many had been worked already but new techniques would be tried. New ores and minerals were always being sought.

Some investors simply wanted claims of ownership or stewardship. If they allowed or blocked access to other mines, fine. If they had even a smidge of mineral potential, fine. Some were located away from others and offered the opportunity to provide new mineral riches, or the appearance thereof.

Whatever the property's attraction, people from many nations would find themselves buying and selling. At hand were actual physical claims as well as stocks and bonds issued by companies owning the properties. These tradings and transactions went on in mining camps everywhere.

ABBY TALKED WITH HER FRIENDS AND NEIGHBORS IN AND around Nederland and neighboring Caribou. The area had been worked since the 1860s. She had no lack of mines, mills, and claims to pick through.

IN DENVER, COW WAS GOING TO SEE PAUL IN HIS OFFICE.

Having come in early, Paul was thinking of a property he had briefly owned several years previous. It was technically a working mine, a surface mine. With a woman he had partnered up and they were ready to cash in. He hadn't thought of Charity Hovus for quite a while. Unbeknownst to his wife, he and Charity had a business going. The two of them thought they had hit the big time and were leaving town together. But someone got to the payoff before they did. The whole deal collapsed and his wife was none the wiser. Paul considered bringing Charity to meet Cow, Carlton.

No, he thought, better to let that matter rest. Carlton could handle business just fine. No need to bring in a new face now. Cow was just doing just fine and didn't need to have a new coworker/competitor to deal with. Besides Paul wasn't sure Chari would consent to talk to him. About anything, much less about business. Their last meeting was icy at best. He would find out soon; he and Charity were having coffee within the hour. Probably better to reestablish cordiality and leave it at that for now. Paul didn't really need nor want another partner now that Cow was working.

He returned to the present as Cow entered.

"You have been busy, Carlton. Central City, Blackhawk, Idaho Springs have potential, no? And a trip to Breckenridge to boot! Lots and lots of claims and properties, some so-so and many, fine. Looks to me like you have gotten us a lot of properties and material to work with."

They shook hands. Cow nodded.

"Yes. You wave an assay report up there and people come out of the woodwork. Buyers, sellers, speculators, you name it. I have lined up a fair spectrum of property ownership."

"Well, Cow, I want to hear about it but have to go out. An old associate and I need to catch up."

"Thanks. Have a good meeting." He waved as Paul strutted out. Cow wondered how many of his old associates were cordial and how many might be angry. Maybe irate, ready to pull a gun. Just what old associate, he wondered. What was Sawyer cooking up? And how would he, she or they, affect him and his claims?

I'll know soon enough, he thought. He opened his case and pulled out a stack of papers. Time to review and report the previous weeks' efforts and conversations. Most of them made him smile.

First document was about his talking with an older, semi-retired miner. Cow opened the conversation.

"Well sir, we can help you. I got to looking at the area and your filing. It seems we own all the claims on that hill. All, that is, except one. Yours. We have access to all of ours but now you don't. We don't really need that one but having it would simplify our records. And your life. We'll pay you and you can retire to Denver or Colorado Springs."

He remembered pushing a paper across the desk towards the man.

"What's that?"

Cow shrugged. "We can relieve you of this problem. Go ahead and read it."

"My mine is a paying property. Why should I sell?"

"Your little mine pays, but not much. And face it, your record keeping is suspect. Are you really profitable? Not to mention that maintenance and exploration are expensive. And access. Can you bring in equipment or crew now, without trespassing on ours?"

"You are choking me all around."

"That may be true. Up to this time we have been looking the other way. But access which we have graciously allowed you is now over. Not a problem for us but you and I need to talk about that."

The man glared silently at Cow who went on,

"Things are tightening up. We may have to bar any crossing of our claims."

"But that means I can't get to my mine."

Cow nodded sympathetically. "True, sad to say. I repeat, we can relieve you of this problem. Just sign here and you will be free of worries."

"Its not enough. And how about royalties for the ongoing income you'll get from my mine?"

"What's that? Make ongoing payments to you? For what? It won't be yours. We won't pay you for access to our own claims, that's for sure."

He leaned forward, put his hand on the form as if to take it back. "This is a generous, one time offer. And it may be withdrawn after today. We will take this dog off your hands and you can take your money and go down the road. Just sign here…"

Cow made it sound as if he and his company had long owned the surrounding claims. What the man didn't know is that they had only recently been bought. Purchases were made in the name of Paul Sawyer or a new partnership or a company. A number of them had been recently set up just for the purpose. These claims, and the buying entities for that matter, were useless, sterile, non-paying as producing mines. But owning those claims gave leverage. They gave control and a gate to give or bar other's access.

The man signed. Cow remembered the anger and hatred in his eyes. Too bad. In his mind, taking control of another mine overcame that hostility.

A FEW DAYS LATER, IN DENVER.

"I'm so glad you're home, Cow. You've been gone a lot."

"Me too, Suze. The mines in Central have kept me busy."

"I thought you didn't want to mine."

"I'm in mining but I'm not actively mining." He held out his hands.

"See? My hands are clean and so is my face. I'm not underground mucking ore or planting charges. I am talking to miners and miners' families. Buying, selling and trading claims and properties. All above ground!"

"Do you like it?"

"Yes. Between you and me. I think I can go out on my own and make a better living. For us."

"Oh Cow. Don't. We are just getting settled here in Denver. I am happy here, with things to do besides avoid saloons and dodge stray bullets like in Cripple. And your children are doing well." She smiled. "They have made some friends and like their classes."

She crossed her arms and looked him square. "Don't you go hounding off after some half baked dream and try to make us move."

Cow shrugged. "Hey, you're right. We're all settling in well. I'm glad we are done dodging bullets, like you say, and I don't need to look over my shoulder for pinks." He glanced at a stack of papers he needed to review.

"Tomorrow I need to go meet Paul. Now Suze, I promise you, if there are any changes on the work horizon you'll be the first to know."

THE NEXT MORNING IN PAUL'S OFFICE, COW SAT BACK.

He had obtained quite a few viable properties. Paul and his partnerships and companies owned a lot more than when he started. The whole deal sometimes bothered him. A little, not much. After all, this was hardball, almost blackmail. What else could one call blocking an owner's legal access to deeded property? Cow loved saying 'we can relieve you of this problem'. The more he thought about it, the more scant became his sympathy. Far as he was concerned, the guy should have bought up the dry claims around him just for protection. Too bad if he didn't and someone else did.

As he sat there basking, he revisited something he and Suze had touched on. He, Cow, and no one else, had obtained the properties for Paul. But his name was nowhere on the documents. Carlton Weston did not exist as far as these mine properties were concerned. He was invisible to the law and to the income derived from the transaction. He frowned at that, and wondered just what to do about it. Maybe he needed to take another look at striking out on his own?

On his own he had come up with another tack, a way to get buyers. Salting. Strewing pieces of paying ore around an otherwise barren site. Cow wondered why that was called salting. Maybe it was from olden days. Salt used to be valuable and was fought over as wealth. Maybe some old camel jockey sprinkled salt at an oasis site trying to lure development, or make a sale of land or to lure an enemy in…

As he sat there he had no idea Paul had experience of his own with salting. The 'associate' Paul had just seen had her own stories and experience about that.

She and some friends made a barren hole look rich with old second class gems. The supposed diamond mine was way out in far western Colorado. She was looking for investors. Paul was one of those people she contacted, folks with money looking for more. After one look Paul decided it was too good to be as advertised.

Shortly after, the two of them sized each other up. Paul left his family and the woman left her partners; they tried to head out with the pickings. That didn't turn out as expected. The woman went her own way and Paul came back to his wife. He was soon running his own investment 'opportunities'.

Cow knew nothing of this. He was pretty sure he had invented a new approach to separating investors from their money. A plan formed in his mind. For now, he decided, he would keep it to himself.

SEVERAL WEEKS LATER HE WAS ON THE TRAIN HEADING WEST. Cow loved working in Blackhawk and Central City. It reminded him of Cripple, lots money, lots of booze, easy come easy go. But this time he didn't have to go down the hole to earn a buck. No premature charge would blow him to smithereens. There were no cave ins or company goons to worry about. Today he would walk and talk the saloons, street corners and assay offices in Blackhawk.

Carlton, or Cow as he still thought of himself, truly liked this part of the job. It was fun and often enough, lucrative.

He would start out soft and easy. In his mind he was just tossing out the line gently jiggling the bait.

"Have you heard? I hear that the (fill in the blank) mine hit a gorgeous rich vein."

Of course he had heard no such thing. But people were willing to talk, to trade gossip and tips. He likely would learn nothing about 'fill in the blank'. Information on other properties and people, he would get. Some valid, lots of it empty.

No matter. Someone would spill a nugget of truth about an abutting claim, or a claim down the hill. Better yet, he might glean news of the mine's owners. Many, not all but many, were in debt. Some just owed on a legitimate loan to dig ore. Some, however, were in over their heads: in gambling real deep, or running around on the wife, in over his head with other claims. Any one of these gave Cow leverage.

One of the best things he ran across was innocent money new to town. There was eastern money, Denver money, London money. All of it eager to buy in on the next big strike. And ready to look past warts and conflicting signs, concentrating on the big payout. Cow made sure they thought it was just around the corner. One more push, one more dollar, and they'd be there!

Over a cup of coffee, of all places, he met a man who went by Red. It was curious because the man looked to have a mixed heritage, dark hair, and his complexion didn't look like sunburn was a worry.

Cow knew better than to ask. How or why the man answered to Red didn't matter anyway. People drifted in and out of mining camps. They'd tell you what they wanted you to know. Most got testy if you pried. Some got downright nasty.

Cow himself practiced that and appreciated that most others did too. His idea was, live and let live; don't ask unless you absolutely have to know. As far as he was concerned, the more people kept to themselves, the better.

"So, Red, you're new to town. And did I understand you to say you may want to invest here in the Blackhawk diggings?"

Red nodded, looking around as he spoke. "Yup. I sure hope the mining is better than the scenery. My God, there isn't a tree for miles. All I see is bare rock, slag piles, mine dumps..."

"Well Red, this camp gets called 'the richest square mile on earth' for a reason."

Cow grinned, then got serious. "You can make a fortune getting ore out of the ground, make it into metals. Trees get in the way of that. Some of 'em get cut for mine support beams and fuel and so forth. So, I guess one can enjoy scenery and starve. Or make money. Which do you want?"

"I was just noticing, is all. I want the ore. And more money. I want a mine. And I have some money I could use for that." He looked around furtively as if to keep it a secret.

Cow worked not to snicker. Whether he knew it or not, the guy just new in town was a sheep looking to be shorn.

"I have some funds. From selling my holdings in Rhode Island, a factory. Well, it is a mill, right on the Massachusetts line, really not a factory. Lots of mills running on the rivers."

He snorted at the memory and the difference from there to here.

"What you westerners call rivers out here are a joke! Even the big ones don't carry enough water to float a child's canoe. Your 'rivers' wouldn't rate being a brook back home. I tell you what…"

"That may be, Red. This is not lush country, I'll give you that. But we have something Rhode Island doesn't."

"Oh?"

"Gold! Silver! Nickel, copper, lead…!"

"Yes, Carlton, you're right. But I sure miss trees and rivers and lakes." He grinned. "But I'd rather have the things you mention than greenery. Now tell me. Do you know of any mines, good ones, up for grabs? I've looked around, talked to some folks, but can't seem to find a good property. I need some help. You seem a solid citizen, an honest man. Maybe we can work together?"

Cow felt the nibble, paused as if weighing and thinking. Then he set the hook.

"Why thank you Red. I try to do right. Matter of fact I may be able to find something for us." He watched to see how Red would take the 'us'. The man didn't react.

"Off the top of my head, there are several possibilities. The Ajax, the Singing Parrot, the Mountain Luck and the Columbina are all in play. Looking for an infusion of cash or for a new owner." Cow knew that some of these mine clams were available and others not. No matter, Red wouldn't know which was which. He went on, a little dramatically. "And…" He paused as if trying to decide whether to add another. "And there you have it."

"What do you mean, 'and'? And what? What else do you have?"

Carlton the businessman made a show of discreetly looked around to be sure no one was listening.

"Well, Red. I don't know. I guess I can share this with you. There is one other property I'm aware of. Word isn't out on the street yet and it looks like as doozy. Strong vein, distressed seller. The owner—original owner—owes a friend of mine money. Big money. The guy has to sell, but no one knows it yet. I've seen samples and they look… wow. Don't tell anyone. I'll trust you with the name. The mine is, get this, it is called the Double Double."

Red tapped the table two times, twice, excitedly. "Tell me more. That sounds like just the ticket."

"Come on over to my shop, Red. We shouldn't talk on this here." He stood and so did Red. "I have some samples and so forth there. And an assay report. Sometimes it is called the Two Double."

Cow, or Carlton, knew but didn't share some things. Again he had little sympathy for this shiny easterner with money and too much trust. As he walked, for a moment he held his breath. There were several items he didn't say, or even dare to think:

The ore samples supposedly from the Double Double were random pieces of very high grade ore, not local to the site.

And that they had been strewn around the site of the Two Double for the right someone to find.

And that the assay report was typed up in Paul's office on letterhead titled for the purpose.

And that if Red didn't bite quick, he knew several other fish hot to 'invest' in the mine.

As they eyed the samples, Cow set the hook. "Do you have money on hand, Red? If this looks like it is for you, we need to move fast. Before word gets out, I mean."

Cow could see by the greedy gleam on Red. The man was in.

"Tell you what, Red. I'll leave you here for two or three minutes. I have some paperwork to run in the next office. Call if you have questions and I'll be right back."

Cow remembered that day well. After their visit to the office, Red gave him two five figure checks.

"Congratulations on acquiring the Double Double, Red. You have made a good decision." They shook hands. "I have some paperwork to catch up with, so will leave you for now. Talk to you soon!"

With that Cow decamped to Denver. Time to let Red sort things out on his own. He relived relieving Red of his money, enjoying that he kept one check for himself. The other would go to Paul as total proceeds. He knew that part of that check too was his, for lining up the deal. All in all a good day!

As Cow heard Paul come in he came out of his reveries. "How was your meeting with the old business associate?"

"Good to catch up." Paul decided to leave it at that.

"Say, you've been busy, Carlton. Thanks to you, we've tied up a number of claims and are seeing results. Some investors are happy to sell to get us out of their hair. Others want to invest in your newly rich mines. Good work!"

"'Thanks. Yes, I have been hitting it pretty hard. I think Blackhawk will be hot for me for a while. Better I not show my face for now. I imagine Red will be looking for me, not in a hospitable way."

Smiling, Paul nonchalantly asked, "Really?"

"Yup. Time to move on, at least for a while. I hear there is a new strike in Boulder County. Nederland and Caribou districts, twenty miles west of Boulder. Maybe I'll hop over and take a look."

XIV

Ben and Abby sat soaking in a fine spring day. He gazed at the sunshine and she looked at a record book. The winter winds were softening, almost meek and pleasant. Crocus and dandelions were poking their heads up along the edges of snowbanks. Daylight was minutes longer every day, earlier sunrise and later sunset A real blessing!

She put down the ledger, the records of each property and how it cost or paid them. It made good reading overall. She meant to say something to Ben. But recent events and efforts which showed well in the records captured her thoughts.

Her thoughts riffled over the months. She had been busy acquiring and tying up mine properties in the region. Some of the year's memories were vivid and some were scantly pictured. There were meetings, negotiations, visits to the land office. Much of the time was spent tracking down owner's heirs.

Several encounters came to mine.

A Denver spinster looked skeptically at Abby.

"Tell me again why you want our old claim, Mrs. McFall? My great uncle John Curry put his heart into that mine. He got nothing out. He came to Nederland sure he would hit it big, this being a silver and gold camp. Brought along my grandparents and parents. Paid them to work in the mine. No matter which way he had them dig, most of what turned up was black sludge, not gold. Curry's slurry, he called it on his death bed. I can't imagine what you want…"

Abby smiled, took a breath. "Well, Miss Curry, we need to consolidate. Your claim, John Curry's claim, is near our Deportati mine. We want to be sure we can easily bring in the equipment we need. Simple access is all."

"I want you to keep the name if I sell to you."

"We can do that. Now, we will pay a nominal amount to clear it out. You'll have no more paperwork or tax liens or any of that. We'll take all of that over."

Out came the company checkbook.

"If you would sign here I will write a check."

ANOTHER DAY ABBY RODE A FEW MILES WEST OUT OF NEDERland through the town of Eldora. Her goal was the nearby settlement of Hessie. Not much was left of that once thriving mine camp. She saw many abandoned structures with just a few cabins in use.

"Hello Mr. Jethro O'leary. I believe you know my husband Ben McFall."

"Yep. He done found the Deportati and is doing well I hear. Too bad I didn't have the luck with my Red Quill mine. Got some gold but a lot of black goop. Curry's Slurry someone called it. Worthless slime gumming up the works."

"Here, Jeth. I brought you a bottle. Old Spike is your brand, no?"

He looked between her and the bottle she held out. Licked his lips.

"What do you want?"

She pulled out a form and a twenty dollar bill. "I want to buy the Red Quill. You sign this, I give you the cash and the Old Spike. And then we go our separate ways."

Jeth took the bottle, opened it, and swigged. Pretended to think for a moment and visibly came to a decision. "I can't write my name. I can just print the initials of the mine."

"Make your mark. I'll witness it."

He took the paper, looked at her. "I trust you. 'Cause you and old Ben wouldn't do me wrong. Here goes!" He made an artistic RQ. Then a shaky X. The twenty disappeared into his pocket before Abby finished signing to witness it.

As Abby left, he called, "Tell old Ben hello. Good luck getting to the good ore through that damned black stuff."

Abby grinned inwardly. If you only knew, she thought.

At first the whole process, buying up claims, kind of kicked at her conscience. It didn't take long to see that the widow Currys and Jethros of the world were better off. Money from Abby and no worries left them in a nicer spot than where they had been. She and Ben too were in a better place.

It wasn't all talking to lonely has beens in old cabins or shacks. One day in Denver she was at a bank. She'd set up a meeting with some sort of representative, of course a man. He was grandly suited, in formal business fashion. She figured he came from the east. He looked a fop. And his disdain wasn't well disguised. The attitude he wore about this dusty cow town was not respectful. He made no attempt to disguise it.

"Well, Mrs. McFall. Is your husband coming?"

She glared. "No. I will review your offering and make a decision."

He paused, nonplussed, then continued. "We under-stand, I understand, that you are looking for property."

The man represented a syndicate—Abby thought it was in Boston but wasn't sure. In any case, it had somehow acquired town lots and mining claims in western Boulder County, Colorado. Probably, he had drawn the short straw for the job of disposing of them. Which was why he was in Denver and not real happy about it.

"We—my husband and I—live in the town of Neder-land. About twenty miles west of the city of Boulder. We may be interested in what you have there."

"Why do you want these properties?"

She parried. "Why do you want to sell them? Just what do you have, and what price are you asking?"

He covered his surprise at the unexpected response by laying out a map.

"We offer seven town lots and eleven mining claims, some overlapping.

She turned the map around, made a show of studying it.

'You have deeds, claim filing papers, proof of tax payments?"

"Of course." He nodded at a briefcase he had carried in. "We are prepared to offer them for one hundred dollars a parcel, eighteen hundred in all. Cash, no financing or terms."

"Eighteen big ones? For a few tiny lots and some over-lapping, unpaying mine claims?"

"Yes. Our research shows that is a fair price for choice residential lots and mine properties."

She smirked. "You're not from around here, are you?"

The price was inflated and both knew it. He nervously rustled the map.

She gazed at the dude for a moment. "We'll offer three hundred ninety nine dollars for it all. And we will need those signed releases, deeds, and all ownership documents." Out came her cash stuffed envelope.

It was less than his syndicate wanted for 'assets' in this isolated mining town. He also knew they wanted no part of old mines nor a random collection of city lots. He didn't want to but would likely take her offer if she wouldn't up the number.

"Make it four ninety nine?" He half muttered, half demanded. Actually he was surprised he said it.

Abby smiled, extended her hand. "Deal. I'll need a separate receipt for cash payment."

SHE RECALLED OTHER TRANSACTIONS AND MEETINGS. MOST but not all of them went her way. Some were downright hostile and unproductive. All in all Abby did well scooping up old mining properties.

ABBY'S MEMORY AND MIND CAME BACK TO SPRINGTIME NEDERland. She looked at her husband, then the ledger books.

"Ben. Last month we turned a corner."

"Oh?"

"The Deportati made more money from tungsten than from gold. Add to that the income from our other claims.

The ones we are just working the tailings for black sludge. Curry's slurry. Or 'that damned black iron' as some old timers called it."

He grinned. "Some sludge! Funny isn't it? You and I have been chasing gold all these years, and silver before that! Who would have thought? And now, we're making it big on a metal most have never even heard of!"

She smiled. "I have to say, Ben, when your train pulled away from Cripple that June day I was scared. I thought I'd probably never see you again. I bet you didn't think we would end up like this, minor mining tycoons. I sure never did!"

THEY SAT TOGETHER. HE SMILED.

"I've been thinking. There's a man in England named Herbert Hoover. An American. Big cheese geologist, worth millions. Made his pile mining in China. I understand he is always on the lookout for opportunities. Like the Deportati. And John Curry's Slurry."

He paused. "How about we go to London this season? There are people over there we ought to see."

Afterword
Notes on Fact and Fiction

BEN AND ABBY, COW AND SUZE, PAUL AND OTHERS WERE CREated to carry the story.

But remember: many men and their families actually experienced the separation, hardships, choices and anxieties these characters had to face.

FROM ABOUT 1890 INTO THE 1920S, A NUMBER OF MINERS WERE in fact shipped out of many western mining camps. Miners (accurately) dubbed the State Militia 'the mine owners' police force'. Those men usually did the dirty work of loading the deportees into boxcars.

The Colorado towns of Cripple Creek, Idaho Springs, Telluride and others in the region experienced this. Union men and suspected sympathizers were forcibly loaded onto trains, taken to the state border and dropped off. From there they were on their own.

Security 'officers' were enforcers hired or contracted by mine owners. Many of them followed or were waiting for the deportees. Their aim was to intimidate and keep the miners away from mining camps.

As long as people have kept animals, others have tried to steal them. Livestock rustling was (and remains) a high risk/high reward business. Tales of summary justice are legion and accurate.

Branding cattle and other stock with red hot iron is pretty much a thing of the past, at least in the US. RFID implants or ear tags have largely taken the place of burn scars to denote ownership. Technology allows the tracking of individual animals, which creative rustlers do their best to work around.

Miners in the Nederland and Caribou districts of Colorado early on found their gold and silver works polluted with a strange dark mineral. As early as the 1860s many cursed and discarded 'that damned black sludge'.

Late in the century someone figured out that the stuff was valuable. Big steel manufacturers such as the Krupps did in fact solicit wolframite and tungsten from Colorado. A second mineral rush was on! District mines accounted for the majority of tungsten produced in the US during World War I.

The mining of investors for money goes hand in hand with mining the earth for minerals. Every one of the ruses Paul Cow and Abby used (and more) were put into practice wherever money, mines and minerals came together. Not to mention railroad, water and land development schemes…

About the Author

Stan Moore is a husband, father, grandfather; a third generation Coloradan; an author and historian; a Vietnam veteran; a retired small business owner; and an avid mountaineer, backpacker and desert rat. Moore and his wife make their home near Denver with their cat who lets them stay there.